WITCH HEALER PRIESTESS OUTCAST

Divine feminine archetypes
for modern life

JULIE PETERS

Illustrated by
Nadia Murash

VERBENA

CONTENTS

OUTCAST

WELCOME

"Myths are like mushrooms", the writer Sophie Strand has said: from the surface, they looks like individuals, with a little stem and curved top poking out from the dirt, all alone. But if you dig a little deeper, you will see a network of root-like threads called mycelium connecting each single mushroom to all kinds of other mushrooms and non-mushroom beings, extending across a wide swath of land.

Each of the divine feminine figures we meet in this book have roots like that, oral and written roots that traversed people, lands, and cultures for centuries, even millennia. Some of these roots have been forgotten, but still they reach up through the dirt to the light, demanding to be remembered.

Once, there were deities of storms, the wild wood, healing herbs, wolves, the ocean, fertility, wisdom, and everything else. The divine world was filled with color and flavor, and it taught us precious secrets about how to survive and thrive on the land. Modern life is busy and technologized, thoroughly separated from ancient lessons about which berries are safe to eat and the rhythms of the wolves in the wintertime. If we can "re-root" these mythologies, as Sophie Strand suggests, we can reorient them to the lands they came from, remembering how they once helped us to live with the plants and animals with whom we shared our space.

I live in a place known in Cree as *amiskwaciy-wâskahikan*, Beaver Hills House, a place where many indigenous bands would gather to rest, trade, connect, and enjoy the many resources of this land. In English, this is Edmonton, Alberta, Canada, a city designed so you never really have to get out of your car and face the extreme cold or blistering heat of the seasons here. I grew up as a (lazy) Christian with English and Irish roots, and while I loved the rituals of church, the spicy smell of incense smoke, the cool hard pews and the thin powdery pages of the Bibles held behind each one, something was missing. I turned to witchcraft as a teen, casting love spells and burying my hair clippings in the garden. I studied literature and world religions at school, fascinated by stories of gods and goddesses that were so different from what I'd learned at church. I became a yoga teacher, and sat rapt at the feet of anyone who would tell me a story about the Goddess in her fierce and powerful forms. Now, as a therapist, I listen deeply to the intimate narratives of my clients' lives, and work to help them re-story their inner worlds, to create new narratives of healing and change.

As in my previous book *Maiden, Warrior, Mother, Crone*, I have dug deep into the rich loam of oral history and written word to find the stories that follow.

THE STORIES AND THEIR SOURCES

While these divine feminine figures are deeply researched (and beloved) by me, I want to be clear that I am not an expert on the religions, living traditions, or the lands or peoples connected to them. It is not my intention to disparage anyone's individual experience of these belief systems, but rather to re-root the spores of the stories that have been obscured through time and politics. The root systems burrow deep, run far, and nourish many wells, but in my experience, these stories are also intimate and real, aspects of our inner selves that have always been and will always be. These stories are new versions, fresh shoots from old dirt. They are intimate and imaginative, but not intended to be authoritative.

Myths usually began as oral tales that were shared and reshared for generations before anyone wrote them down. They once lived in the mouths of their storytellers, shifting and changing depending on the audience, and risked death in the coffin of the written word, no longer able to shapeshift with the people who needed them.

And yet, it's often thanks to scant written records that we still have these stories at all. Historically, the writers were the victors, the people in power, the ones with a voice that could echo through the ages. The writers decided which stories stayed and which would be deleted, burned, edited out. And yet... an inscription here and there, a lingering curse against an enemy, even a magic spell hidden in a clay jar for centuries can recall the goddesses the writers tried to erase. Though this evidence is static, frozen in runes, letters, or cuneiform, it comes alive in our imaginations, in our fantasies, and even in the arguments of scholars who can't decide what these old scripts really mean.

My academic training taught me to seek information in books and research papers, and while I've done that here, I also immersed myself in podcasts. I listened to conversations, often in the voices of the people who live within the traditions and on the lands of the stories I wanted to know. Podcasts are cutting-edge storytelling technology, a reclaiming of orality in a world dominated by the written word, and many of these storytellers brought new perspectives or information that I couldn't find in books and papers.

FOUR DIVINE FEMININE FIGURES

The **Witch** has been many things over the course of history: a shapeshifter, a rebel, a midwife, a servant of the Devil. But really, she (or he or they) is someone who pays attention, who listens and learns from the world around and within them. A witch's magic comes from the audacity to *know* without needing permission.

The **Healer**, from the Old English *haelan*, is "one who makes whole." The healer connects body and mind, spirit and culture, being and land. They can see the whole picture, dig into the system's roots, and recover those missing links.

The **Priestess** holds divine secrets. Her work is to remember the stories, to share them with those who want to know. She stands at the veil that separates us from the Otherworld, and, if we're willing, initiates us into that hidden place.

The **Outcast's** power threatens those who command order. They unsettle the borders that benefit the powerful and so are cast to the edges. There, they practice the magic of disruption, of remembrance, of forgotten inner powers. They remind us of the magic that rests with the unknown, the lost, reviled, and feared.

As the Witches, Healers, Priestesses, and Outcasts in this book came alive for me through my research, they whispered secrets in my ears, infiltrated my dinner conversations, and appeared in my dreams. So here they are, together with images – the new iconography – by the brilliant Nadia Murash, who illustrated in conversation with what I've written. As you turn these pages, I hope these divine feminine figures find yet another new life in your imagination, your dreams, and your storytelling. You are now a part of this mythic mycelium. Welcome.

A NOTE ON THE MEDITATIONS

With each chapter of this book, you are invited to integrate each story with a meditation. You can do these meditations in any way that feels right as long as it's safe for you, your people, and the land.

Acknowledge the land that you are on and your relationship with this land. Consider where your family and people came from, as far back as you're aware, and how you made it here. Notice the quality of the light today, the season, the weather, and the phase of the Moon. Remember yourself as an integral part of the web of everything.

You may also want to consider the land of the goddess or divine feminine figure you're working with. Think about where that is or was in the world, if you've ever been there, if you have ancestors from there that you know about, and if the land has other names that you know of. Notice how thinking about that land, that climate, or that part of the world resonates with you as you think about it now.

Then imagine a circle of protection around you. You can do this literally if you like, with salt, stones, or chalk, but it's not necessary. Set the clear intention that only energies that are in alignment with your highest good and the highest good of all may enter this circle; anything that is not in that alignment stays outside of the circle. Light a candle, if you wish.

When your meditation is complete, thank the land, the circle, the goddess or divine feminine figure you've been working with, and anyone or anything else you'd like to offer gratitude towards. You may also like to journal after each meditation, letting your own writing add to the tradition of these stories. Make them yours.

HEKATE: GODDESS OF WITCHCRAFT

In the dark of night, as the Moon slipped into the void between stars, Hekate stood at the crossroads. Her three heads shifted in and out of view, sometimes appearing as one, sometimes appearing as three, all attentive, watching, listening. The whisper of the wind stroked the trees. The ground slithered quietly with worms, snakes, and the spirits of the long-dead. Hekate's ghosts wept and cried out in fear, desperate for some understanding of their deaths, the meaning of their lives. There were too many to comfort at once.

Hekate stood, still, watching for the signs. A caterpillar sat snug in the cocoon that would turn it into a butterfly. Frog larvae squirmed restlessly in the pond. A strawberry flower, swelling at the center, was nearly ready to become sweet, pink flesh. All was right, then. And yet something had changed, some smell in the air or sound in the wind not yet made material. Hekate did not move.

Hecuba, the goddess' loyal dog, sniffed the air carefully, a shiver passing through her soft black fur. Hekate looked at the dog, eyes still so human, for she was once a queen of Troy, driven mad by the death of her sons after her city's fall. She was a good warrior, a good queen, fierce. So when the queen began barking and howling like a dog in her grief, Hekate transformed her into this shape and took her on as a companion and consultant. The animal's madness came in handy from time to time.

And then she heard it. A howl of pain and panic, a sudden rush from the earth, and then a strange quiver from the tree roots. Hecuba yowled as if she had been waiting for this, her old keening bellow set the ghosts to it as well, a cacophony of sorrow. Someone had entered the Underworld. Someone who did not belong there.

Hekate lit her torch, wishing to see further into the darkness. The ghosts settled, always soothed by its warm light. Hecuba lifted her nose and bent her legs, ready to spring forward, waiting for instructions, trusting her mistress would know where to go. Hecuba always wanted to *go*, to *fight*, to *find out*. But this strange sound felt like nothing Hekate had heard before, and she had been listening for a long, long time. She put up one finger, indicating that they would not be chasing this night. She wasn't sure why, but Hekate knew they needed to wait. Hecuba whined a little, but settled.

For the next ten days, Hekate waited. She followed her ghosts to Demeter, goddess of grain, whose grief was to the ghosts as a flame to a moth. The goddess' daughter had gone missing, and her heart was broken. Demeter's hands had gone cold, her usually richly golden hair streaked with an unfamiliar white. As she wept, her cold tears salted the earth, stopping the flow of life from the Underworld that should rise up as fruit and grain. Hekate lit Demeter's dark paths as they searched for her daughter all day and all night, the world shriveling underneath her every step. Demeter's lovely world, once so abundant and alive, suddenly seemed woven through with death. Hekate felt deeply for her friend, but waited, understanding that something was happening in deep time that Demeter's grief could not allow her to see. Still, with ten days gone by, Hekate could no longer stand to see Demeter so distraught. Her sorrow was like an unslakable thirst, as if her heart were six feet below her body at all times.

"My friend," Hekate said gently, "there is one place we haven't looked." Demeter looked at her friend, her icy blue eyes rimmed red from unceasing tears. Hecuba leaned her head into Demeter's leg, the dog offering her warmth and empathy, knowing the grief of a lost child all too well.

“I do not know for sure what happened. But the night Persephone went missing, I heard a strange sound, like someone entering the Underworld, where they should not be. I fear that is where she is.” Demeter’s eyes went black and hard as if she already knew.

“Take me there,” she said, her voice grave.

“You know I cannot,” Hekate answered. “You should never return. And the world needs you, as is clear,” she gestured to the desiccated trees around her, the frozen pond, the caterpillar cocoon fallen to the ground like nothing but a dead leaf.

Demeter nodded, her jaw set. “Go to her, then, Hekate. Comfort her. Tell her I am coming.”

Demeter set off for Olympus to speak with her brother Zeus. She would remind him of her power, which was older than his, and that without her participation, the human world he loved would wither and die like the leaves on the trees. She would find a way to get her daughter back, Hekate knew that. She trusted in her friend’s power.

Hekate felt for the keys in her pocket. She found the correct one, golden, its ring held on a soft red ribbon. She stroked its curves and ridges and slid it into an invisible lock, conjuring the gates of the Underworld as she did so. As she slipped softly into the realm of death, she wondered if Persephone would see the magic in its dark corners, understand the beauty of composting death preparing for its return to the light. She never knew for sure if Hades understood the world he now ruled, the world that was once hers. Hekate had not seen the need to fight for this realm, as Hades had left plenty that needed ruling, such as the thin veil between death and life, the moment when an infant moves through the portal of breath, the graveyards, and the crossroads, where even Hades could not see in the three ways. Hekate would not abandon her people, the ghosts, the lost ones in the in between, and the dead. They needed her to be able to traverse the boundaries between life and death, just as they must. Hekate walked deeper into the darkness, her beloved dog and the procession of ghosts following silently.

To her surprise and delight, Hekate found Persephone rapt with curiosity about this world. She attended to the voices of the dead, listening more than she spoke. She calmed and soothed them, tending them like so many green shoots, just emerging from the earth. She felt the ghosts calming, drawn to Persephone's warm tenderness. Persephone turned, noticing her mother's friend, and immediately collapsed in tears. She ran to Hekate, who wrapped her arms around the girl. She seemed so young and slight now, when just moments ago she had appeared so powerful and strong, as if she belonged in this dark, cold realm. Hekate could feel how much she missed her mother, how confused she felt, how much grief she was absorbing in this dark place. She had the instinct to love it like Hekate and Hades did, but she had a lot to learn. Hecuba settled, resting her soft body on Persephone's bare feet, placing her head gently on her paws, her eyes sleepy.

"Can you take me home, Hekate?" The girl asked, her eyes filled with tears.

"I cannot, my dear," she said gently. "But I will stay with you as long as you need me." Hecuba nudged at Persephone's hands, wanting to lick away her salty tears. The ghosts had paused, their attention fixed on the two women, as if waiting for a command.

"I can teach you, if you like," Hekate added, her eyes on the ghosts. "This place could use you, I think." Persephone's eyes widened. The girl was, indeed, at a crossroads: she belonged here, in some way, but she also belonged with her mother. Hekate did not know how to reconcile these two truths, but she knew the magic Persephone would need to do her work down here.

From this time, the two women worked together, with Hekate teaching Persephone the secrets of soothing the dead, helping them settle into their new reality. By the time Hermes appeared, sent from Zeus to bring Persephone home, she wasn't so sure she wanted to go. Hekate saw the look she gave Hades, the longing, the feeling that she wanted to see her mother again but did not want to leave forever. She drew the girl and the god of death away from Hermes.

"I have a spell," she offered. "'The food of the dead'." Hades' eyebrows lifted. "If Persephone eats a little, she will be tied to this place forever. Zeus dare not keep her from her mother for long, but there are more powerful energies than even the King of the Gods."

Persephone looked to Hades, shyly, and he looked back.

"I would very much like for you to stay with me, Persephone," Hades said, "to rule the Underworld with me as queen. But I will not keep you from your heart's desire."

"Six pomegranate seeds should be enough," Hekate offered. "For six months of the year. You can stay here with Hades and myself. I will teach you whatever you need to know. When the time comes, I will guide you myself back to the Above World and your mother."

Longing, loss, hope, and confusion crossed Persephone's pure face.

"You are learning the powers of darkness," Hekate told her. "They can bring balance and justice, a reminder of the power of death in the world of life. I believe there is rightness in your place here. But it is up to you, my sweet girl."

Persephone's eyes shadowed, and she suddenly looked older and wiser, less the maiden she once was and more the queen she was becoming. "Six pomegranate seeds," she agreed. Hades offered her the fruit, and she took the blood red seeds from his hands, the juice filling her mouth with life, death, and rebirth, all at the same time.

So it was agreed that Persephone would spend half the year in the Above World with her mother, and half the year in the Underworld as Hades' queen. While Demeter grieved in protest, causing cold and quiet winter to fall across the land each year, Hekate had found a companion in her work, a powerful witch to help her attend to the howling ghosts and the keening lost souls that followed her nightly. Persephone became her first student, but she would not be the last. Today, her students are legion, and Hekate is known as the goddess of witchcraft.

HEKATE: QUEEN OF DARKNESS AND LIGHT

Evidence of the goddess Hekate (also spelled Hecate, usually pronounced *HECK-ah-tee*) first appeared in Anatolia in Asia Minor around the sixth century CE, but likely existed in oral tradition long before that, possibly even in connection with the older Egyptian goddess, Isis. Her famous sanctuary at Lagina, in modern-day Turkey, included a temple, a House of Priestesses specifically for her female followers, and the Nymphaeum, a fountain dedicated to the water spirits called nymphs. Pilgrims would travel there to pray to the goddess and perform elaborate rituals including herbs, potions, incantations, and divination – essentially, ancient witchcraft. Several curse tablets, which were ancient spells written on thin pieces of lead, have been found buried or in pots, sometimes with bits of hair, little dolls, and other items, invoking Hekate's name. The tablets would call on the goddess to help bind an oppressor or enact revenge.

Hekate was adopted by the ancient Greeks and became a part of the Olympian family, but was always slightly outside the main pantheon of gods and goddesses. In some stories, she was a Titan, and participated in rescuing Zeus from his father, who had swallowed all of his children due to a prophecy that one of them would overtake his rule. Hekate handed Zeus' mother, Rhea, the stone that Cronus would swallow instead, allowing Zeus to rescue the other children and kill his father, creating the Olympiad and becoming King of the Gods.

Hekate is Trivia, the one who can see in the three ways. She stands at the crossroads, which in Roman times would have meant where three routes diverged, able to see in all directions. She carries the torch that lights the path forward, and she holds the keys that open the gateways between the worlds. As the original witch, Hekate presides over the *pharmakeia*, a word that refers to both medicine and poison – a given substance can be either, so you'd better make sure you're getting it from the right witch!

Many ancient goddesses easily held the binaries of life and death, love and fear, fertility and barrenness, good and bad fortune, or summer and winter within them. Later patriarchal belief systems began to separate these concepts into light and dark, good and bad. Some people believe Hekate was once a form of Artemis, the virgin goddess of the hunt whose cult was once ubiquitous. When Artemis began to shift into a "light" goddess, Hekate became a separate figure, able to hold the "darker" qualities that were once integrated into the goddess as a whole. But Hekate has also been called "tenderhearted," collecting ghosts and unsettled spirits to her. In her book *Hekate: Goddess of Witches*, Courtney Weber names her "the goddess of all that has been rejected."

WORKING WITH HEKATE

While this great witch-goddess was strongly suppressed during the rise of Christianity, she had a resurgence during the witch-hunting of the early modern era. Here, she was invoked as an evil crone, an ugly old woman who would kill and eat children. Despite this vigorous attempt to blacken her reputation, Hekate is enjoying something of a third incarnation now as the patron goddess of modern witches and pagans. People today feel a draw to remember the magic of the old ways, and Hekate is just the guide to help them do that.

Hekate is the goddess of the crossroads, whether literal or metaphorical. When you don't know whether to go right, left, or straight ahead, Hekate will stand with you, torch lit, helping you see the way forward. She will not tell you what to do or do the work for you, but she will be by your side. So much of witchcraft is about listening inwardly, paying attention, using our senses to trust that part of ourselves that *knows*, without needing someone else to tell us what to do. Hekate's torch can help light our way.

MEDITATION WITH HEKATE:

Keys at the Crossroads

Classically, Hekate was honored with the *Deipnon*, a supper held at the crossroads on the night of a new Moon. A simple way to practice this today is to leave some food or drink at a crossroads near you. Ensure that it is safe for local flora or fauna and/or well wrapped so that someone who might be hungry can come upon it and enjoy it. Do your spell or meditation here, or simply imagine a crossroads as you drop into your inner knowing. The following meditation will help you navigate a crossroads: a situation where you have a decision to make and aren't sure which way to turn. Acknowledge the land you are on. Consider Hekate's lands, ancient Greece and Anatolia, and all the places she's traveled since then. Imagine a circle of protection around you, inviting only energies in alignment with the highest good.

Imagine two paths that you could go down. Name one "staying the same" and the other "changing." Contemplate the first: the path that is closest to the status quo, closest to the patterns that are familiar for you, that would require the least change for you. Notice how you feel in your body when you imagine yourself walking down this path. Notice any thoughts or feelings that arise. Then attend to the second path, the path that feels more like changing, where you would need new skills, to draw on unfamiliar parts of yourself or where you'd need to ask for more help. Notice what it feels like to imagine yourself walking down this path. Can you see a third path, an alternative direction, or perhaps the option to do nothing at all?

When you're ready, invite Hekate to join you here. See her in her three-headed form, able to see in all directions at once. Welcome her, honor her, and indicate your offering to her. Imagine her lighting her torch, and simply witness with her, let her see what you've gleaned from these possible paths. She may or may not indicate a direction, perhaps handing you a key to pass through a portal. Stay with her as long as you need to. When this feels complete, thank her, thank the land, the circle of protection, and your own ability to see with your mind, heart, eyes, and body.

MORGAN LE FAY: SORCERESS OF AVALON

Morgan took a bite of the juicy apple she was holding in her hand. It was sweet, crisp, and tart, with a taste she'd never been able to find in the Otherworld. She leaned against the knotted wood of the apple tree's trunk, surrounded by its soft pink flowers, which blossomed alongside the fruit no matter the season here in Avalon, the Isle of Apples. She breathed deeply, inhaling the scent of her home, the sweet smell of rich dirt, flowers, and composting fruit. She finished her apple, gently pressing its seeds back into the earth before rising to visit her sister.

Morgan walked to the edge of the lake, her bare feet collecting dew from the soft fresh grass, and waded in, quietly singing the song that she knew would call Nimue to her. Morgan felt her legs shimmering, a deep desire rising within them to transform into the tail of a salmon. She dove like a mermaid into the cool, clear water, allowing herself a moment of deep, shivering pleasure when her legs at last became a tail. She continued her song under the water until she could see her sister Nimue, a blue-green mirage in the sweet waters of the lake.

Nimue's face was ethereal and pale, ringed by soft blonde hair glimmering in the water. The two embraced warmly and then Nimue took Morgan's hand.

"I have much to show you, sister. Come."

The two swam deeper into the lake, at last coming upon the mirror that could show the truth, the past, and the future. Nimue touched the mirror reverently, and Morgan watched as images from the Otherworld came into view.

She saw an Otherworld version of herself, human, a child. Her chubby face was framed with wild strawberry curls, and she wandered the woods joyfully.

Then she saw her human mother, Igraine, combing her long dark curls, her blue eyes flashing. A man Morgan didn't know was looking at her with lust and desire, a strange cruelty in his eyes. He turned his gaze to another man, a man who looked familiar, almost like someone Morgan knew from this world. His long beard was askew, his hair tangled, and his eyes wild but intelligent, brimming with knowing beyond knowing. A magician. A handshake and a promise between the two.

Then she saw her mother's belly swelling, pregnant, but not by her husband.

And then Morgan saw Igraine's husband, Morgan's human father, a sword piercing his chest in battle.

Morgan exhaled. She was both living that life and not living that life, and she felt all of its feelings. Her tears mixed with the waters of the lake.

"There is great change afoot in the Otherworld," her sister told her, holding her hand gently. "You must help the little boy growing in your mother's womb. He will have great power."

Morgan shook her head.

"You've always known you had work to do in that world, my Morgan," Nimue said, her long fingers gentle on Morgan's cheek.

“I don’t think I like that world very much,” Morgan’s green eyes turned away from the mirror, looking for her friends, the salmon and herring, to comfort her. A silver eel, tasting her tears, slid around her tail fin, a blessing and a comfort.

“I know, my love. But our world is connected to that world for good and for ill. It needs your wisdom and power. Without you, it will become purely a world of men’s power and we will lose all the old ways.”

Morgan didn’t like it, but she understood. She and her sisters had been here for millennia, in the ageless time of the Isle of Apples. But the Otherworld shifted constantly around them, and from time to time they needed to intervene. Morgan turned her attention back to the mirror, and its images returned.

She saw her human self, older now, in the strange habit of the nuns of the Otherworld’s God. She was learning human magic: mathematics, reading, and astrology.

Turmoil flashed around the peace of the nunnery. The evil king who had stolen her mother was growing old and sickly, dying before the baby, now a young man named Arthur, was old enough to take the throne. England without a king: chaos.

Then she saw the strange magician creating an illusion involving a sword and a stone that somehow convinced the people young Arthur was to be the rightful king.

“This is how he gains the throne?” Morgan asked incredulously.

Nimue laughed lightly. “These are the games of men. Merlin is a skilled illusionist.”

“The madman?”

Nimue chuckled. “Some say that.”

Morgan stared at the image. “He’s like us,” she said to Nimue.

“In some ways,” her sister agreed. “In other ways he is very different. They say his father is a demon from some other land.”

“Is it true?” Morgan asked. Suddenly the man in the mirror appeared to be looking directly back at her. She gasped.

The vision shifted again, and the human Morgan was at the court of her little brother, Arthur. She saw herself healing his knights, providing him counsel, working with the madman, Merlin, her magic growing by the day.

The visions faded. That was all they would see today.

Nimue squeezed Morgan’s hand. It was time to join her Otherworld self. The rest had not yet been written.

“I will be here if you need me,” Nimue told her, embracing her tightly. Morgan allowed another tear to slip into the lake waters while she held her sister, and then steeled herself to return to the surface. As the sun touched her skin and as her tail reached the sand, her legs returned, her toes squishing pleasantly into the lake mud. She blew her sister and the lake a kiss, its surface calm and quiet.

She returned to the apple forest and wandered reluctantly until she found what the Otherworlders called a fairy ring, a circle of bright white mushrooms in the grass. Morgan stepped inside.

In a blink, Morgan found herself in a vast field of bluebells, the petals brushing her bare ankles. The world was carpeted with them, turning the forest floor violet, filling the air with the flowers' sweet, almost spicy scent. Her human memories and emotions flooded in as time shifted strangely, the past and present rearranging. She felt herself both of Avalon and of this Otherworld. She breathed in the bluebell fragrance deeply, adjusting to the dizziness of time and identity.

Morgan felt for her magic – still present but a little grainy on the human side, taking a bit more effort. She transformed into a black cat, her nose close to the bluebells as she returned through the field of flowers to the castle. She padded lightly along the long hallways until she heard a familiar sound. Arthur's wife, the striking and dour Guinevere, was up to something in her chambers. Morgan peered around the threshold, curious.

The queen was burning buttercups and rosemary, muttering words under her breath and making the sign of the cross over her heart. She was attempting a spell, but it was nothing like Morgan had seen before, whether in Avalon or with the magician Merlin. There was an image of a sad-looking woman in blue holding a small child framed on what appeared to be Guinevere's altar, and she was fingering a long-beaded necklace with a cross at the end. Morgan perked her cat ears, listening.

"...take away my love for Lancelot so that I may be faithful to my husband Arthur. Amen," Guinevere finished her prayer. Morgan startled, losing focus on her cat shape, and awkwardly appeared in her full human form, right there in Guinevere's private room.

Guinevere gasped, her face open and shocked at the sight of her sister-in-law. The two stared at each other for a long moment.

Morgan opened her mouth. "Barley would be better than buttercup for that, sister. And you need some salt."

Guinevere started to cry.

"It's all right, Guinevere. We all have love and lust for many people. It does not make you a bad person. Lancelot is lovely, and handsome enough. I've seen the way he looks at you," Morgan did not need magic to know these two were desperately in love. They could barely conceal it even in front of her brother. Guinevere cried harder.

"Arthur has his dalliances. Does it really matter if you do, too?" Morgan stepped closer and attempted to place a hand on the poor girl's shoulders, a hank of her dark hair freed from her normally perfect braids, but Guinevere flinched.

You know it is different for men and women," she said sharply. "I should not need a spell. But I am desperate, and one of my handmaidens told me to try this."

"Spells are lovely when they work. They are not the only kind of magic," Morgan said gently. "I could teach you if you like."

Guinevere recoiled. "Don't you know what they say about women who practice magic? That they are evil, that they don't believe in God, that they... fornicate with the Devil," the girl whispered the last part, as if afraid anyone would hear her.

Morgan laughed loudly. "I suppose you mean what they say about me, then?" Guinevere blanched, then reddened. Morgan's laughter faded.

"Arthur knows I am helping," she said quietly. "I do not care what others think." Guinevere looked away. Clearly, the queen did not share that sentiment. Morgan saw that this was not to be a moment of thaw between the two women. It had been cold between them since she'd arrived at court, and she had never understood why. Perhaps this innocent Guinevere thought she was fornicating with the Devil.

"Well then," Morgan stood, smoothing her dress. "I will leave you to your privacy. I apologize for interrupting you." She turned to go, then added, "your secret is safe with me."

The two women never spoke privately again after this. Morgan felt for Guinevere at times, suffering needlessly when Morgan would happily have helped her unite with her love. Morgan could see why she was so torn, however, as rumors and hearsay became more and more intense against anyone who still practiced the old ways.

Things took a turn for the worse for Morgan when her older sister, Morgause, appeared at court and managed to get herself pregnant by the king, likely through some enchantment. Rather than assuming Morgause was simply trying to secure a place for herself at court, the people blamed Morgan, believing that she had organized this situation with the intention of planning her brother's downfall. This infuriated Morgan – she had been sent to this ugly world to help her little brother, not to depose him.

As the rumors got more and more lurid, Morgan felt the fear and vitriol extending to all women of this Otherworld realm. In Avalon, she and her nine sisters ruled the land peacefully and playfully. Women had power and access to the mysteries, and while the faeries had gotten a bit of a reputation for playing a little too hard with the humans from time to time, they never really meant harm unless harm was done to them or the land. Here, women were being called witches as if that was a bad thing, accused of killing and eating babies, and doing all sorts of disgusting things with demons and devils. As Morgan continued to help and advise Arthur, and heal his men when needed, people saw her skills as more and more evil and dangerous.

She spoke of this to Merlin. "I am only doing the magic I know as well as what I was taught by you and the nuns, and they think I am evil," Morgan told him. Merlin listened, but did not reply.

"You know they say you were born of a devil," Morgan added.

Merlin laughed, but did not deny it. He dropped a little bit of what looked like fire into some potion he was working on, and it fizzed and bubbled.

"You are as much of a witch as I, and they do not attack your character. You are the king's most trusted advisor. Why should I not be the same?"

"I am a scientist," the wizard said, stroking his long, tangled beard.

"You are a madman," Morgan shot back, and Merlin chuckled again.

"That too," he said softly.

"I don't like the way this feels," Morgan said. "I do not feel anyone understands me here, perhaps not even you, Madman." Morgan paused, feeling tears threatening. "I miss my sisters."

Merlin looked at her. "No one is keeping you here."

Morgan felt dismissed. Merlin had orchestrated the death of her father and the birth of her brother all by magic, and no one was accusing him of fornicating with the Devil. This week Morgan had heard someone suggest she was old and ugly beneath her courtly clothes. Another had whispered that she could shoot fire from her nether regions. An awkward place to shoot from, at the very least, since she could do it with her fingers. She'd seen a few other women, simple hedge witches, healers, and midwives without much real magic publicly humiliated, tortured until they admitted the ridiculous things they'd been accused of, and then hanged or burned at the stake anyway. Morgan did not like the way things were going in this human realm. And she wasn't sure she was making things any better.

So it was that one night, in the dark of the night, she stole from the castle in the form of a field mouse. She ran past the castle walls to the heath, where the normally purple heather appeared an uncanny shade of blue-red, the dark of a fresh wound. She pushed through the coarse bushes of yellow gorse, a burnished gold in the moonless night, until she found what she was looking for. A wild rowan tree, growing alone on the heath, its clusters of bright red berries signifying autumn was coming. Morgan shifted back into her human form so she could press her hands against the tangle of thin trunks intertwining. She was surprised to find a tear traveling down her cheek. Even this tree, this clearly magical tree with its tiny five-pointed stars on each berry, which had been used for generations in magic and ritual, was now being used to ward magic *away*. Morgan wept for the world as it was changing, the loss of the old ways, the fear and the cruelty that even her brother showed to women from time to time. She wept for Guinevere, who was so afraid of her Roman God she never trusted Morgan once, who could have been her friend, her sister. She couldn't help but feel she was returning home a failure.

As Morgan opened her eyes, she found herself by the same rowan tree, but now its red berries nestled ripe alongside clusters of white flowers, looking cheerful and almost fuzzy in the dusky light. She was home. She sat by the tree and wept all the tears she had for the life she was leaving behind, for this human Morgan who had tried her best, but had not been able to change the tides of the time. After an endless while, she fell asleep, and dreamed of Lancelot and Guinevere, her brother and his many enemies, Gawain and the other brave knights who did not seem cruel of heart, who did not seem to want to hurt the world. She dreamed of a great sword, gifted to Arthur by Nimue, with a scabbard that would keep him safe. Morgause's child Mordred, taking the scabbard and wounding Arthur mortally with the sword.

When Morgan opened her eyes again, she was surprised to see her sister sitting with her, her blonde hair gently stirring in the soft breeze. She so rarely saw the Lady of the Lake on land, as she much preferred the world of water.

"You were crying out in your sleep," Nimue said gently, turning Morgan's face, swollen with tears, to her own kind blue eyes.

"I have failed, sister."

"There is no success or failure," Nimue said simply. "You have done your best."

"That world has become poisoned. I am afraid of what the people will do with magic, with women who practice it. They want to forget the old ways."

"You have helped them remember it. Even if their children call you a demon." Nimue smiled gently as if all was well, a little mirth behind her eyes. "All time has its time. Your seeds have been planted," she said. "And, my darling sister, your task is not quite finished."

Morgan slumped. She did not want to return to Arthur's court and the bleakness of his world.

"One day Arthur will need your help again. You will bring him here," Nimue said.

"Here? But this is not his world," Morgan protested.

"You will know when the time comes. There is a reason you are his sister. He will come here at the moment of his death. We will welcome him, and he will come to understand."

Morgan looked at her sister, hoping for more of an explanation than this, and knowing that, as usual, she likely wouldn't have one.

"Come, sister. Would you like to swim with me?" Nimue took Morgan's hand in hers, soft and gentle, tugging her towards the lake. Morgan smiled, relief in her shoulders.

"Yes, my sister," she said, rising to her feet, craving her tail. "Let us swim."

MORGAN THE FAIRY

Morgan Le Fay first appeared in writing in the 12th century CE, with Geoffrey of Monmouth's *Vita Merlini*, "The Life of Merlin." In this story, Morgan is a goddess of the fae world, maybe even the Celtic goddess the Morrígan, who was also a shapeshifter with something of a dark reputation. Morgan could also have been a mermaid – her name, *morgen* in Old Welsh (which later became Muirgen, referencing an Irish mermaid legend), means "sea born."

In the *Vita Merlini* and other related tales, Morgan rules Avalon with her nine sisters, nine sorceresses or, possibly, virgin priestesses who guard a great cauldron. They are healers, shapeshifters, and in some stories they can breathe fire. Morgan is their queen, and altogether they receive Arthur after he is slain by Mordred, leaving the possibility that the great king could one day return to rule again.

As time went on, however, Morgan's image shapeshifted. Like Hekate, she got a severe witch-washing during the witch-hunt era, when she appeared in stories where she would be clearly evil. But she never totally went away, and she is still beloved to this day, even including her darker aspects. She still appears everywhere from Disney's 1963 film *The Sword in the Stone* to Marion Zimmer Bradley's 1983 book *The Mists of Avalon*, which was adapted into a miniseries in 2001. In all these works, Morgan remains ambiguous, often retaining some of her benevolent goddess-like qualities along with a little of her nefarious flavor.

MERLIN THE MAGICIAN

Merlin is a fascinating character in his own right. His name means, essentially, "madman," and as the legend goes, he was the product of a nun and a demon, an incubus sent by the Devil to try to create the antichrist to fight the powers of the good. The nun, however, found a priest to baptize Merlin before his birth, thus rescuing him from the powers of evil. Despite this dubious beginning, Merlin doesn't get nearly the poor reputation Morgan does for being a witch!

MORGAN AND THE MODERN WITCH

To this day, witchcraft is feared by some and embraced by others. Some still see it as a devil's practice, while others work with it as a radical embrace of knowing and power outside of patriarchal religious control. Like Hekate, Morgan refuses to be categorized, to be pinned down as just one thing, and that's part of what makes her so powerful and resonant even today.

Modern witchcraft can follow a specific religion like Wicca but it doesn't have to. It can also be a simple practice of listening to intuition, paying attention to the land and the seasons, and performing simple rituals that help us understand ourselves and what we're going through a little better. It can be a way of resisting the systems of oppression around us simply by insisting on being who we are, rather than who someone else tells us to be.

As an ancient Celtic goddess, Morgan would have presided over the energies of light and dark, birth and rebirth. These deities didn't need to be "good" or "bad" because their power involved both. Morgan is ultimately a shapeshifter, a goddess of the Otherworld, and, perhaps, a human being with the same flaws and limitations as the rest of us. She can hold all those realities at once without being limited by any single one of them. The important thing is not what we're able to accomplish or how other people talk about us. The important thing is that we know who we are.

MEDITATION WITH MORGAN LE FAY:

A Glimpse into the Mirror

Scrying is an ancient witchcraft practice of peering into a dark or clear surface to see the truth or the future. Stereotypically, it's a crystal ball, but witches have used mirrors, dark stones, calm bodies of water, or even the darkness behind their own eyes to do this work. As we enter into a gentle trance state, we open our inner seeing. This can be practiced anytime, but close to Halloween (October 31st) or Samhain (around November 1st) is traditional.

Prepare for your meditation by finding a quiet, dark room and your scrying material of choice. Acknowledge the land you are on as well as Morgan's lands, which include England, Scotland, Ireland, and Wales. Set a circle of protection around you, being very clear that you are only inviting energies in alignment with the highest good, and anything that is not in that alignment may not enter the circle. If you wish, set an intention about what you would like to see. What question do you need to ask? What do you really want to know? What energies or information do you wish to invite today? A simple intention could be "I wish to see for my highest good and the highest good of all."

Stare into your scrying surface and listen to your breath. Let your eyes go soft and receptive, but keep your attention in the direction of the scrying surface. Notice any images that arise for you. If you'd like, speak the images out loud. Allow your energy to be about receiving, not "trying" to see something.

Imagine that Morgan Le Fay is with you in this practice, perhaps the both of you are underwater, with salmon tails, in Avalon's magical lake. Listen to her and honor anything she wishes to show you.

Stay here as long as you'd like. Honor and thank your guides, Morgan Le Fay, the land, the circle of protection, the scrying surface, and your own inner seeing.

GUAN YIN: GODDESS OF COMPASSION

Once upon a time, a beautiful princess named Miao Shan lived in a grand castle with a powerful king and queen. On the day of her birth, flowers rained from the sky and a great rainbow appeared. The people saw this as a sign that this princess was special, destined for great things.

The king, however, did not care for prophecies. He was only interested in the power of his kingdom and was greatly disappointed that his youngest child was born a girl. He already had two daughters, who were beautiful, kind, and obedient, but all carried the great flaw of being girls.

While Miao Shan's sisters obeyed their father's every wish, the youngest princess could not help but disobey. She had a peculiar quality about her, which was that she was curious. She liked to wander away from the castle to the laurel-leafed forests, especially on days when the whole forest was blanketed in fog, as if she was walking through a cloud. She would listen for the insects and animals around her, hearing all their sounds. She even felt their feelings, tuning into them when the light touch of a butterfly's feet graced her outstretched fingers, its dusty luminescent green and blue wings flashing in the dim light, or when a green tree viper wrapped itself around her arm as if she were nothing but a tree branch, allowing its tongue to taste the air around her. When she returned home and was punished for her wanderings, she'd simply meditate on all she'd learned from the animals and the trees while she scrubbed the floors or was made to sit alone without her supper.

Every night, Miao Shan dreamed about her past lives. She was Avalokiteshvara, a great *bodhisattva* who had devoted his existence to easing the world's suffering. She was a housewife who cooked and cleaned, simply to make the world a little better for her family and community. She was a gentle and kind king who helped his people live well in accordance with the nature spirits. She was a little boy living his life on the streets, missing his mother and helping his friends. Then she was a snow leopard, a tiger, a frog. When she woke in the morning, she knew this life was no different. She would devote herself to the suffering of others and make it better in any way she knew how.

One day, as she wandered the markets in the humble dress of a servant, she saw a man who was doubled over and coughing. He was ill. She felt for him and wished she had medicine that could help. She offered him a cup of clear water, but it did not cure his coughing.

The next day, she saw an old woman, wrinkled and hunched, walking with a cane. She rushed to help the woman walk, but it did not cure her bent spine.

On the third day, she saw a funeral procession walking past. A dead person and their family, dressed all in white, their faces somber. Miao Shan felt their sorrow and loss and found herself crying with them, abundant tears falling down her cheeks, but it did not bring their loved one back to life.

When she returned to the palace, her father confronted her.

"It is time for you to choose a husband, daughter."

"I should like to marry, father," a smile began to soften the king's hard features, but she continued. "But only if my marriage will ease the three misfortunes."

"What do you mean, child?"

"The three misfortunes: illness, aging, and death. If my marriage eases these troubles, I should very much like to marry."

The king grew cold. He did not intend his daughter to marry a healer. He needed her to marry a future king, one who could wage war, protect the border, and build wealth, not soothe the troubles of the common people.

"That is not what marriage is for, child!" he boomed.

"Then I should like to go to a nunnery and study so that I may help the people myself," Miao Shan spoke meekly.

Shocked by her defiance, the king sent Miao Shan to the gardens behind the castle and restricted her food and water until she learned to obey.

Miao Shan did not complain. She loved the gardens, enjoying the quiet rush of the willow trees and the crawling ants on the peonies. She would help the garden attendants, learning to care for the plants of the garden, drinking dew from the climbing roses and eating the ripe pomegranates and jujubes that burst with scent and flavor in the garden. She would get lost in meditation for hours staring into the sacred lotus flowers, and her sisters would find her so still from time to time that sweet sunbirds would be resting on her head and shoulders as if she were nothing but a tree.

This only outraged the king further. Miao Shan's sisters and mother begged her to listen to her father and marry so that she could return to her life as a princess. She smiled kindly at them and held their hands in hers, but did not budge. Finally, the women turned to the king, pleading with him to grant her wish and allow her to go to a nunnery. Her two older sisters already had appropriate matches and the kingdom was in no danger. The king agreed at last, but with a new plan. He sent her to the White Swallow nunnery, and instructed the nuns on pain of death to treat her poorly and give her more tasks than she could handle so that she would be forced to return home and give her father his appropriate deference.

Miao Shan gratefully attended the nunnery, ready to learn all she could to help whomever she came across. The nuns were standoffish, reluctant to be outwardly cruel but afraid for their lives of what the king would do if they were kind. They piled the most difficult tasks on the girl, giving her impossible amounts of wood to chop and water to carry. Miao Shan worked without complaint, remembering that the Buddha taught that there were great lessons in chopping wood and carrying water. Still, the tasks were insurmountable, and she could not get enough done between sunrise and sundown.

One day, at the edge of the forest, she collapsed, unable to carry her unsustainable load. A black bear came across her crumpled body and recognized her right away. The bear returned to her family in the forest, and they took pity on the girl, taking on her load of wood, chopping it for her. When Miao Shan awoke, she found her tasks completed, a soft black bear sitting next to her, warming her with her fur, waiting for her to wake up. She bowed deeply to this bear friend, thanking her and her family for their assistance.

The bear returned to her family, and Miao Shan was alone. A strange fog settled around her. She listened as the cloud forest thickened and thinned, feeling beyond its blindness, sensing a great being nearby. From the land clouds emerged a beautiful orange head, striped with black. Her amber eyes were locked on the girl, and she snorted lightly. Miao Shan bowed deeply to the tiger spirit, filled with reverence, empty of fear. The great tiger bowed back in recognition, then turned around and disappeared again into the mists.

The next morning, a beautiful spring had appeared right next to the nunnery's kitchen. The wood was chopped, and fresh water was immediately available. The forest had helped Miao Shan to complete her tasks. The nuns looked on in awe and surprise, and, forgetting their promise to the cruel king, hugged and praised her, seeing that she was truly connected to the magic they studied every day.

Miao Shan lived happily with the nuns for only a short time before her father heard about these miracles. The king grew enraged, and beneath that, there was terror of his daughter's power. He decided she must be killed.

When the executioner appeared, Miao Shan was attending the monastery garden, which had flourished even in harsh weather under her gentle hands. He shot an arrow at her, but it broke and fell to the ground before it hit her. Miao Shan looked up, and saw the man approaching her, sword in hand. She saw the fear in his eyes and knew right away that he was sent by her father. She knew that if he failed to complete this task for her father, he would be killed, but if he succeeded, he would suffer from the terrible karma he would accumulate from this act. It was an impossible choice.

The executioner raised his sword, and it slipped uselessly from his hands, piercing the ground instead. Terror filled the man's face. He ran at her in desperation, his hands grasping at her throat. She closed her eyes and prayed to take on the man's karma for him, letting him be free in her stead. She allowed him to take her life force in exchange for his heavy load of karma.

All of a sudden, Miao Shan was in a very dark place filled with shadows. She heard the cries of suffering and fear all around her, the ghosts of those who had died with the deeds that they must atone for before they could be reborn. Her tears flowed and her heart expanded with care and worry for these creatures and their suffering. From her body, a gentle light emanated, illuminating this dark place. Her tears soaked the ground, and fragrant flowers grew at her feet. The ghosts settled, calmed by her light in the darkness, and she began to sing to them, a lullaby to allow them rest in their troubled afterlife. She offered them all the good karma she had accumulated in her many lives, and began to set them free from their karmic debts.

Before long, the death realm began to look something like paradise. The guardian of this realm could not abide this lightness and sweetness. This place was meant to be for atoning and learning, for casting off the karma of cruel choices. If Miao Shan stayed much longer, she would upset the balance of the universe. So the guardian called to the tiger spirit to help. The beautiful being who had met Miao Shan in the forest appeared and invited her to ride on her back, returning her to the above world. When they arrived in the forest outside the nunnery, the tiger spirit bowed to the princess and offered her a gift: a rare Peach of Immortality. She bowed deeply in her gratitude, vowing to devote her eternal life to easing the pain of the suffering.

Many years passed, and Miao Shan's father, the king, became gravely ill. He knew his body was showing the signs of the many cruel and unfeeling choices he had made to gain power and riches, which couldn't help him now in his suffering. He regretted treating his daughter so cruelly, ultimately causing her death. He began to settle himself to the punishment of his life, filled with fear and resignation about the hell realm that waited for him. Worried, the queen found a nearby monk to see if there was anything that could be done to ease the king's pain.

"There is one way to cure this illness," he told the king and his family. "If you can bring me the eyes and arms of one without hatred, I can cure what ails you."

The king laughed. "Who in this world is without hatred?" he groaned in the pain that his laughter caused.

"There is one, Your Highness," the monk offered. "A bodhisattva who resides on Fragrant Mountain. She has vowed to help anyone who needs it, and she will help you."

The king did not believe he deserved such healing, but the queen insisted and he was in no state to resist. So they sent the monk on to Fragrant Mountain to make their request of this beloved bodhisattva.

As promised, the monk returned with these precious gifts taken from the bodhisattva's body and brewed them into a powerful potion. The king drank, and found his ailments, both body and soul, soothed, cleansed, and cleared. He began to cry tears of gratitude and sorrow, feeling the pain of all the cruel choices he had made and the kindness of the one who had deemed him worthy of healing. The king and queen resolved to visit this mysterious bodhisattva and thank her themselves.

The moment the royal couple arrived on Fragrant Mountain, they felt the sacredness in the soft, salty air and found themselves pausing in reverence to the thousand-year-old gingko trees that grew there. As they climbed the mountain in search of the great healer, the fog settled gently over their shoulders, blanketing them in mist.

When at last the queen and king found themselves at the feet of the great bodhisattva Miao Shan, her eyes and arms now gone, the queen fell to her knees in shock. She knew her right away.

"Daughter!" she cried, grasping at the young woman's feet, tears filling the wrinkles of her face, her heart full and broken at once. "I never thought I would see you again!" Her emotion broke through her voice in a rush of feelings she had been forced to hide since her husband had decreed her daughter's death.

Miao Shan stepped off her seat and knelt on the ground beside her mother, feeling her sorrow and confusion through her tears.

"I am all right, mother. I am where I have always wanted to be. I learn and meditate all day. The great gods, the animals, the plants, and the sea are my teachers. I work to heal the three misfortunes every day of my life."

The king spoke: "You are not all right! You gave your eyes and arms to me, the one who always tried to prevent you from doing as you wished, who ordered you dead! I did not deserve the gift you gave me!" Despite himself, the king's tears were dripping to the earth below him in great puddles. He fell to the ground, anointing his hands and forehead in the holy water accumulating on the temple floor.

Miao Shan rose from her mother's side and stood to her full height.

"Father," she said softly.

He looked up at his now mutilated daughter.

"I had no need of what I gave to you." Suddenly, Miao Shan's eyes sparkled like diamonds, becoming thousands, able to see beyond seeing. New arms sprouted from her body, becoming thousands, able to do the work of helping the world. Miao Shan had become the goddess of compassion, the immortal bodhisattva *Guan Shi Yin*, She Who Hears the Suffering of the World.

The king and queen bowed deeply as they watched this miracle, their daughter become eternal, a goddess able to help the world in ways they never had. As they watched her ascend to the heavens, her physical form shimmering into eternality, the king and queen knew that they must devote the rest of their lives to acts of goodness, teaching, and supporting their people rather than their own power. Guan Yin healed their pain, their suffering, and their cruelty, not with her arms and eyes, but with her compassion.

GUAN YIN: SHE WHO HEARS THE SUFFERING OF THE WORLD

Guan Yin, which is also spelled Kuan Yin, Kwan Yin, Quan Yin, Quan Am, and Kannon depending on where you are in the world, is beloved throughout East Asia and internationally. She began as Avalokiteshvara, a male bodhisattva from India around the fourth century CE. A bodhisattva is someone who has attained enlightenment through Buddhist practice, but instead of ascending to heaven, they decide to remain in some form that can help everyone else gain enlightenment.

When traveling monks brought these ideas from India home to China, they gained great popularity, and Chinese Buddhism developed along its own path. The story of the princess Miao Shan appeared in the 11th century CE with *The Precious Scroll of Fragrant Mountain*, a text usually ascribed to a monk called Jiang Zhiqi. This story has taken on a life of its own, influenced by Buddhism, Taoism, and indigenous Chinese folklore.

Classically, the Buddha, who was born a prince, was prophesied to become a great ruler or a great teacher. His parents tried to shelter him, hoping he would become a king, but one day he encountered the Three Misfortunes: sickness, old age, and death. This inspired a lifetime dedicated to easing the suffering of humanity. One of the foundational Buddhist teachings is that pain is inevitable, but suffering is optional. Compassion is the medicine: removing judgment allows the pain to be what it is without piling suffering on top of the situation.

AVALOKITESHVARA'S TEARS

In a famous legend, Avalokiteshvara cries for the suffering of the world. From the tear in his left eye appeared White Tara, a beautiful, calm, gentle, compassionate goddess who could assist him in his work of liberating the world. From the tear in his right eye was born Green Tara, a fierce goddess ready to step into action to help in her own way.

It's not totally clear how the male Avalokiteshvara became the female Guan Yin, but some believe he thought a woman's form could be more useful for those who needed compassion. The distinctly feminine Guan Yin also appeared during a time of strict and intense patriarchy in China. Even when the gods are very powerful, the people always need a goddess, and here she is, as Guan Yin, ready to hold us even when no one else will.

WORKING WITH GUAN YIN

Guan Yin will see the good in anyone, anywhere, anytime. Like Hekate, she will even take on the restless ghosts who are in hell for doing very bad things. She doesn't care who you are or what you've done. If you are suffering, she will be there for you.

Miao Shan's story teaches the healing capacity of compassion, especially for her father, whose body and heart she heals through her sacrifice. She also teaches the power of nature and paying attention – lessons we see in parallel tales like Cinderella, Vasilisa, and Rumpelstiltskin, where young women are forced to complete impossible tasks and need the help of the spirit world to do so.

Perhaps my favorite element of Miao Shan's story, however, is her resolute insistence on listening to her own intuition, even to the point of defiance. She would have made her life much easier if she'd simply married as she was ordered. But something in her knew that was not her path, and despite the trials she faced, she calmly stayed true to what she knew inside herself. As sweet and loving as she is, she is also brave, even rebellious. Guan Yin knows her own power, even when others tell her it's not there.

MEDITATION WITH GUAN YIN:

Mindful Compassion

This meditation is inspired by a classical Buddhist meditation practice that can be incredibly powerful for working with, rather than against, our emotions.

Acknowledge the land you are on and consider Guan Yin's many lands as well. Now begin to contact an emotion you've been struggling with: sadness, anger, desire, or whatever else has been causing you suffering. Call up the emotion and any stories that come along with it. Feel it as fully as you can in your body and notice the physical experience that comes with the emotion.

Imagine Guan Yin here with you now. She is kind and gentle, able to hear the cries of your heart in this moment of suffering. She only sees your humanity; she does not judge you. She has ultimate compassion for what you are going through. With her by your side, allow the stories about the emotion to fade into the background. Especially allow stories of criticism, fear, self-hatred, and so on to be held gently by Guan Yin so you don't have to. See how fully you can still feel this emotion without the stories associated with it. What happens to the sensations in your body when you are no longer judging how you feel? Does the emotion survive without the inner narratives *about* that emotion?

When this feels complete for you, focus your attention on Guan Yin. Take some time to offer her your listening, your attention, and your gratitude. She may have more to teach you here, and she may simply want to be with you. When you're ready, thank Guan Yin deeply for being with you in this moment of suffering.

OSHUN: ORISHA OF THE SWEET WATERS

At the beginning of time, there was only sky and a vast expanse of ocean. Olodumare, the supreme God, lived in the sky with their *orishas*, four hundred plus one beings that represented different aspects of Olodumare's power. The orishas lived happily under a baobab tree, enjoying a life where all their needs were met.

But one orisha, Obatala, was different from the others in a peculiar way: he was curious.

Obatala would peer down through the mists of the world in the sky to see if he could look at the waters below. From time to time his brothers and sisters would find him laying belly down in the sand, listening for the world below. It whispered wild secrets, soothing words, and the powers of Olokun, the great orisha who presided over the wild deep ocean below.

When his curiosity grew great enough, Obatala formulated a plan to create land down below so that he could visit and explore this world. He gathered all the gold he could find in the sky and fashioned a long chain that he slipped through a hole in the above world, reaching down to the ocean below. Obatala climbed carefully down the long chain and found himself at the very end, swinging in the breeze, but still very high up away from the ocean world. He remembered his snail's shell full of sand and released it, sending a white hen after it. The hen landed on the sand, scratching and pecking, spreading the sand, creating the great hills and valleys, the beginnings of the land.

Obatala let go of his chain and landed on this newly formed earth, which he called *Ife*. He planted palm trees and made creatures out of clay, offering them to Olodumare to breathe life into, creating people. All this was good until Olokun, goddess of the deep waters, discovered what had been done to her wild territory. Her rage overflowed, and she flooded the land, sinking the palm trees and drowning many of the people Obatala had so carefully made. Only a few people, gathered at the tops of the highest hills, survived, and prayed to Olodumare for help.

Olodumare heard the people's cries, but they also respected Olokun's rage, as she had not been consulted in these changes to her territory. The great being understood that a new balance must be reached between land and sea. So they selected seventeen orishas to travel down to the earth below and set the land right, creating a balance between Olokun's wild waters and Obatala's land, where the people could live, eat, dance, and make love.

The sixteen male orishas immediately began to clear groves for themselves, creating spaces to work, and discussed with each other how they would approach their project. But they ignored the seventeenth orisha: Oshun, the youngest, and the only woman among them. They did not create a space for her. They did not consult her in their decisions. If she tried to speak, they dismissed her.

Oshun wondered how they planned to do their work without her, but decided to keep quiet, waiting to see what they would do. She knew her power and her place well enough, but it appeared her brothers did not understand it at all.

So she picked up her comb, beaded with coral, and worked at hair-plaiting, the sacred duty of parting the hair and attending to the *ori*, the great spirit of each individual, held in and around the head.

She waited and waited for her brothers to come to consult with her, but they did not. They asked her to plait their hair, making them look kingly and powerful. They would sit in her chair and tell her all about their plans, complaining about what was going wrong, but when she tried to open her mouth to share her perspective, they silenced her. After a time, her patience began to wear thin. Her belief in her brothers dwindled, and she felt rage arising in its place. She completely withdrew her *ashe*, her life force, from the land and retreated to the cool light of the Moon, where she would plait her own hair and admire herself in her mirror, nursing her hatred and resentment alone.

Back on Ife the other orishas struggled to maintain order. Oro attempted to drive away sickness from the people, but fevers soared and an epidemic raged. Shango threw thunderbolts and raised great storms, but no rain would fall and wildfires ravaged the land. Oko attempted to grow food and medicines from the earth, but only ashen stalks drifted listlessly in the wind and dead pits fell fruitlessly into the sand. Obatala tried to create more people, but all he could come up with was piles of lifeless dry clay. The orishas could not understand why their missions were failing so badly.

So they traveled back up to the sky to discuss the problem with Olodumare. They explained and complained and Olodumare looked among them silently.

At length, the supreme being asked the group: "How many of you did I send to Ife?"

"Sixteen," all agreed, counting their heads, looking among each other, nodding.

Olodumare watched them silently, waiting for them to understand.

"Sixteen of you are here before me. But how many did I send to the land?"

"Seventeen," one offered, remembering the one they had left behind, the beautiful woman, the one who would plait their hair.

Olodumare looked at them again. The supreme being blinked.

"Do you truly think I sent Oshun with you for no reason? Do you think you can create anything without the power of a woman?"

The men reddened with shame. They thought of the beautiful and sweet Oshun, her gentleness when plaiting their hair, the wisdom behind her smile they'd never thought to consult. They hung their heads.

"You will need to apologize," Olodumare said. "You will need her help. There is no other way."

The orishas returned to the land and could not find Oshun there. They searched the marshes and the edges of the ocean and could not find her there. They traveled the skies and the edges of the above world and could not find her there. Finally, they traveled to the Moon, and found her at last, alone and lonely, plaiting her hair and admiring her face in the mirror. They surrounded the young orisha and all the men bowed low, their palms open, jewels and riches falling from their crowns and out of their hands. They offered her their heartfelt apologies along with gold, honey, yellow sky flowers, and handfuls of money, pleading with her to help them complete their tasks on the land. She received their apologies and adorned her hair and clothing with the gems and gold they offered her. She allowed them to praise her beauty, wisdom, and power. And when she had had enough, she stopped them, graciously agreeing to do what she had known she was destined to do in the first place.

The orishas returned to the land together, and Oshun opened the sweet, cool waters of the rivers, the brooks, and the tributaries of the land. The hot earth was cooled by the gentle flow of water. The rain returned, nourishing the crops and allowing the food and medicines of the earth to grow. The people's fevers were cooled and the epidemics healed. Fertility was returned to the people, and they were able to create more of themselves through seeing each others' beauty, taking pleasure in each other's bodies, and nourishing new children in the sweet waters of their wombs. All was right with the world again, and the orishas learned never to disrespect or underestimate the ashe, the power, of a woman ever again.

OSHUN: HEALER OF THE SWEET WATERS

Oshun originates with the West African Yoruba culture which dates back to at least 500 BCE. While most West Africans today practice Christianity or Islam, some communities have held onto the old ways – many of which are matriarchal – or are reclaiming them now. As a creation myth, the story expresses a foundational belief in the ashe, the power of women, that should never be ignored.[1]

During the massive displacement caused by the slave trade, many Africans were forced to leave their home and land. Through this exile, Oshun (and other traditional African religious concepts) followed the people, finding ways to hide within Christianity, the religion of the enslavers. Today, many of these elements are incorporated into the syncretized religions of Cuba, the US, and throughout the Americas. Oshun is sometimes known as Oxúm or Ochún, and often as a version of the loving and forgiving Roman Catholic Virgin Mary.

In the Yoruban belief system, Olodumare, also sometimes called Olorun or Olofin, is a genderless supreme being. It is said that there are 400+1 orishas, which are emanations or maybe children of Olodumare, a number that essentially means countless. Each one represents an element of the natural world. Shango, for example, presides over thunderstorms and lightning. Oya, his consort, is an orisha of death and rebirth, as well as the sharp winds of change. Eshu is the orisha of the crossroads, a messenger god and something of a trickster, recalling the Greek Hermes and Norse Loki, as well as our crossroads goddess Hekate. Orunmila is the prophet, the diviner, and is sometimes associated with Jesus, the son of God. In the story, Obatala recalls Skywoman, the Haudenosaunee creation myth of Indigenous North America, where a woman of Skyworld falls through a hole in the sky and creates the land on the ocean world below her from a handful of dirt.

HAIR PLAITING

In the Ifa divination verse that the story is inspired by, Oshun is the "preeminent hair-plaiter with the coral-beaded comb." In Yoruban belief, one's ori is the essence of the self, the orisha of the soul, wisdom, destiny, and the higher self. Hair can be seen as an expression of one's highest self, and is highly significant in terms of how we relate to ourselves and how we present ourselves to the world. To this day, hairstylists and hairdressers should be treated with respect and honor as they hold one's ori in their hands. Oshun does what appears to the male deities to be a simple domestic task without realizing its foundational power.

Oshun's colors are gold and yellow, and she loves honey, which is both sweet and medicinal. She is also associated with the peacock and the vulture. In one story, she flies to Olodumare for help in the form of a peacock, and in her journey the sun burns away her beautiful feathers. By the time she arrives, burned and half naked, she looks more like a vulture. Olodumare takes pity on her and invites her and the vulture to always be messengers between the earth and God. As the embodiment of beauty and love, Oshun also contains ugliness and loneliness. She is both the beautiful peacock as well as the unpopular vulture.

WORKING WITH OSHUN: FERTILITY AND HEALING

If you wish to begin a relationship with Oshun, there are many ways to do that with appropriate guidance and care from someone qualified within one of her many traditions. It is recommended that you work with a teacher and be initiated into her worship rather than doing it alone. In fact, some would warn you not to try to contact her directly without help because you might spark her formidable rage!

Whatever your background, however, Oshun touches on the human condition – specifically in its feminine aspect. Feminine energy is something that exists within everything and everyone. It is the energy of water, emotion, flow, movement, and that which animates the masculine. This story reminded me of one from the Shakta Tantra tradition from India, where a group of gods are unable to complete their work and pray desperately for Shakti, the feminine principle, to help them. When she appears, they bow themselves low, gems and riches falling from their crowns, understanding at last that the world simply doesn't work without a balance between masculine and feminine energies.

Like Guan Yin, Oshun holds the feminine space of calm, creation, and, in some cases, the healing tears of compassion and grief. Oshun's waters can bring us back to a state of balance where, like her, we can create life, fertility, creativity, and forgiveness. Ultimately, part of that healing is about humbling ourselves, bowing ourselves low to all we don't understand, and welcoming the power of the feminine principle within ourselves.

MEDITATION WITH OSHUN:

Healing Sweet Waters

Have a glass of cool water with you for this meditation, or do it while bathing in the tub or your favorite river. Acknowledge the land you are on as well as the land of your ancestors. Consider Oshun's many lands and waters, both in Africa and throughout the African diaspora. Settle yourself and take a few deep breaths, calming and cooling your body.

Imagine a stream of cool, healing water pouring over your head. Imagine the water gently glowing gold, soothing any excess heat or inflammation in your body, calming any illness or unwellness. Feel the healing waters fill the space of your womb or your sexual organs, imbuing them with the energy of fertility, possibility, and the flow of pleasure and beauty. Drink the water with these images in mind.

Invite pleasure as a healing energy into your life. Bring balance with joy and softness, enjoyment and sweetness. Settle any anger you may feel against meeting your own needs, asking for what you want, and remembering your fundamental life force energy that is valuable and belongs in this world. Invite your feminine aspect to arise to the surface and allow it to teach you something.

Notice if any fear, distrust, or judgment arises as you engage with the feminine aspect of yourself. Simply notice those emotions arising, and offer them to the power of the feminine flow all around yourself.

Imagine Oshun in your mind's eye. See her beauty and her wisdom. Bow to her in gratitude and honor, offering your thanks, respect, and attention. Listen to her carefully. When this feels complete, thank her deeply for her attention and care.

AIRMED: GODDESS OF HERBALISM

Once upon a time, great clouds of mist rolled into then north of Ireland. From the mist emerged a great and magical race of people who called themselves the *Tuatha Dé Danann*, the children of the goddess Danu. Among these were Dian Cecht, a magician and healer, his daughter, Airmed, who was wise, intelligent, and intuitive, and her brother Miach, who was kind, creative, and canny. The siblings were even more powerful when they worked together, sometimes even surpassing the powers of their father, the great healer of the Tuatha Dé Danann. Airmed and Miach were not interested in competition, but only wanted to learn together and advance the magical craft of healing.

The Tuatha Dé Danann had found a beautiful land with deep marshes, rich mosses, trees that bore fruits and berries, and clean air with the scent of the sea at the shore. Airmed loved to explore this land, watching the apple trees, apparently dead in the winter, growing flowers in the spring, and then bright with juicy fruit in the late summer. She would explore the magical properties of the rowan and hawthorn trees, finding medicines in their bark and portals to the Otherworld just beyond them.

Airmed and Miach would watch Dian Cecht perform his healing miracles, learning everything they could about repairing wounds from battle, curing fevers, and preventing illness using magical tools. Together, the siblings discovered that there was magic in the land itself – in mosses and fungus, the bark of trees, the foods of the earth – and explored how these could add to the ancient wisdom of their father.

One day, their people entered a great battle against the Fir Bolg, invaders from the faraway land of Greece. In this great battle, the Tuatha Dé Danann king, Nuada, had his hand severed, a blemish that invalidated his kingship. The Tuatha Dé Danann prevailed nonetheless, and the Fir Bolg were contained to the region of Connacht. Still, Nuada could no longer be king.

Dian Cecht set to work. He crafted a beautiful new hand for Nuada from silver. Nuada was able to grip, move, and hold his sword aloft. It was an extraordinary hand, maybe even better than the original. But it did not change the rules: Nuada was still ineligible to lead the people. The great king took this in his stride, grateful he could still at least fight for his people with his lifelike but mechanical hand.

Airmed had a bad feeling as she attended the ceremony crowning Bres as the new king. His mother was Fomorian, from a race of giants who felt they had a claim on this land. The Fomorians had a stormy quality to them, and they didn't always treat Airmed's beloved herbs and roots the way she would have liked.

One day, she discussed her feelings with Miach, who shared her beliefs. "Sister," he said, "I think we might be able to heal Nuada's hand. Perhaps then he could be king again."

"I have been thinking the same thing, brother," Airmed replied with a smile, having already gathered the most powerful herbs she knew.

The two put their heads together and worked, beginning to grow flesh and bone, a real hand that would restore Nuada to full health and thus the ability to reclaim his throne. When they were ready, they approached the former king and suggested their plan. While Nuada loved his silver hand, he knew Bres was not the king to lead his people. He offered his severed stump to Miach, who recited these magical words:

"Joint to joint,
Bone to bone,
Sinew to sinew,
Skin to skin."

As Miach chanted, Airmed handed him bulrushes, blackened in a fire. Over the course of nine days and nine nights, Nuada's hand regrew: the skin, the bone, the joints, and the sinews. At last, the hand was recovered, and Nuada was again free of blemish, restoring his ability to be king.

Airmed and Miach ran to their father, excited to share the news of what they'd done – a new leap in the magic of medicine. But Dian Cecht did not take this as they expected.

In a fury, Dian Cecht raised his sword against his son and brought it down on his head, splitting the skin. Miach looked at his father in shock, quickly healing himself from within.

"Father!" Airmed cried out.

But he did not seem to hear her, caught up in a jealous and irrational rage. He struck his sword down on Miach's head again, splitting the bone.

"Stop! Father!" Airmed cried again, trying to pull Miach away from his father as he healed himself again from within.

This only enraged Dian Cecht further, and he struck his son down again, this time injuring Miach so deeply he could not heal himself.

"No physician can heal that wound," Dian Cecht said proudly, leaving his daughter speechless and in tears.

The great healer buried his murdered son in the dirt and left him there.

Alone at the grave, Airmed cried. She had loved her brother as he had loved his sister. They had only been trying to build on what their father had taught them, learning to use the magic of the land itself, rather than the tools Dian Cecht had brought with him. They had restored Nuada as king and strengthened the people against the Fomorians. Airmed couldn't understand why her father was so angry he would become a kin-killer – the worst crime anyone could commit. While she was glad she'd avoided his sword, she couldn't help but resent a little that her father thought Miach had done this magic all on his own. Miach was a threat to their father, but Airmed was not?

Airmed continued to weep as she contemplated this experience, trying to understand how to live in a world without her beloved brother. But as she wept, a strange thing happened. From the earth Miach had been buried in, herbs began to grow, watered by her tears of love and loss. Purple sage, thick green comfrey, bright yellow dandelion and more – a total of three hundred and sixty-five herbs, each for a specific healing purpose. From Miach's death came a beautiful new rebirth.

Airmed laid out her cloak and carefully began to categorize each plant and its use. She was so deep in her concentration she did not notice her father approaching, finding her at the work of healing in new ways, continuing to defy him as her brother had. He made a guttural sound, startling Airmed, who jumped up. Dian Cecht took hold of her cloak and violently jerked it away, scattering the herbs to the winds, undoing all of Airmed's work.

Father and daughter stared at each other, Airmed's tears drying with the heat of a new anger, a new defiance. She stood her ground, refusing to break eye contact with her father, known as the god of healers. He was not so interested in healing after all, Airmed realized, but power alone.

"Are you going to kill me, too, Father?" Airmed nearly spat the words out.

He paused, staring at his daughter, the air around them filled with fluttering, fragrant herbs, now useless in the healing task. A blush of shame began to redden his chest, rising to his cheeks, as he began to realize what he'd done. "Though Miach no longer lives," he said, his voice breaking as his eyes drifted to the mound of dirt that was once his child, "Airmed shall remain," he finished. With that, he turned and walked away.

The words felt threatening and apologetic at once. Airmed drew herself up tall. "No matter, brother," she said to the grave of her beloved Miach, "I remember all the herbs and their meanings. I understand the gifts of your body, of your death. If someone wants to know how to use them, they must listen with their hearts and I will share with them the *awen*, the deep knowing, and they will come to heal. He is Dian Cecht. But I am Airmed."

With that, the new goddess of herbalism, Airmed, gathered her cloak and set to work.

AIRMED: HEALER OF THE LAND

The legends of the Tuatha Dé Danann, a phrase that means "folk of the goddess Danu," originate in pre-Christian Ireland with orally shared tales whose mythic (if not historical) origins date back to around 1700 BCE. No one knows for sure if these were a real people or purely myth, and the same goes for the Fir Bolg, the "people of bags" who apparently brought bags of dirt from Greece with them to invade Ireland, and the Fomorians, the "warriors of the Otherworld" who were said to be giants or spirits somewhat similar to the Tuatha Dé Danann.

After a series of battles, the Tuatha Dé Danann were finally defeated, sending them into hiding in the *sídh*, the Otherworld, the land of the fae, where they are said to still reside, able to interact with the human world from time to time.

There is a hidden story within this story[2] that reaches back into other myths in other lands. The word "miach" (pronounced *mee-ack*) in old Irish means a measure of grain, like a sheaf of wheat. The word "airmed," which is also sometimes spelled airmid (pronounced *air-rih-vid*) is similar, representing the container that would hold the grain. "Dian Cecht" (*dee-an kekt*), the great healer of the Tuatha Dé Danann, likely means something like "the eager plough." Dian Cecht ploughs the land, slicing into Miach, creating the measure of grain that Airmed then counts and categorizes.

In Egypt, where the Celts once traveled and settled, it is said that Isis, the goddess of magic, was in love with her brother Osiris, who is the god of agriculture and the underworld. Osiris' brother Seth killed Osiris and sliced his body into pieces that he then scattered across the land. Isis gathered the pieces of her brother's body and brought him back to life long enough to conceive their son Horus.

In some stories, Isis sits by the Nile river, just as Airmed sat by Miach's grave, and cries, her tears causing the annual flooding that irrigates the crops and brings life back to the land. In one ritual held at the ancient Osiris festivals, a mound of dirt would be sown with seeds and watered with Nile water. When the grain sprouted, Osiris would be reenacting the agricultural death/rebirth cycle we see here with Miach and Airmed.

Life and death are close relatives here, as well. Later in the tale of the Tuatha Dé Danann, Miach returns to life. Airmed and Dian Cecht have reconciled somehow, working together to create the great Well of Slaine, the Well of Wholeness, into which Airmed placed many specialized herbs. The well is a place where wounded and even dead soldiers can be placed and brought back to health. In the story, Airmed stands with her father and her two brothers, Octriuil (also known as Ochtriallach) and a perfectly well Miach, his mortal wound apparently healed, all chanting over the magical well.

There is a well in County Sligo in Ireland called Ochtriallach's Cairn that is said to be the original location of the Well of Slaine. Another, the *Tobar na nGealt*, or "Well of the Mad" in County Kerry is said to have magical healing powers, especially for mental health. Recent scientific analyses of the well water found high levels of lithium, a mineral that's used in many modern medications to help treat mental illnesses such as depression and bipolar disorder. So perhaps there's a little truth to these magical myths after all.

WORKING WITH AIRMED

Airmed is the daughter of a great healer, so her talent is, to a degree, in her blood. But her abilities, gained in part from listening to the land and her own heart, quickly surpass her father's. The concept of *awen* in Welsh, Cornish, and Breton means something like inspiration, intuition, or creativity, and was translated by the Christians as "the Holy Spirit." Airmed will help anyone who wants to listen in this deep way, to tap into inner knowing and connect to greater spirit.

Airmed's story is also one of grief, loss, death, and rebirth. What happens to Miach reflects the ancient divine feminine cycle, the deep knowing that endings are necessary to create new beginnings. Airmed can hold the emptiness and darkness of loss and stay with it long enough to see the seeds planted there grow up to the light. She is a goddess of herbalists, doctors, midwives, and healers, but also of anyone weeping at the grave of a dearly beloved.

MEDITATION WITH AIRMED:

Healing with Awen

Healing is a practice that uses whatever tools are available, whether they be herbal, mechanical, pharmacological, psychological, or intuitive. Consider something you want to heal, whether a physical or emotional ailment, and we will connect with Airmed's *awen* to see if it can teach us something.

Acknowledge the land you are on and take some time to consider Airmed's land, ancient and modern Ireland. Close or soften your eyes and begin to turn your awareness inward.

Take a few moments to simply receive the darkness behind your eyes and the relative stillness of your body. Quiet down and listen.

Imagine Airmed with you. She is gentle and kind. She pays attention. She listens. Allow her to witness you as you turn your attention to your wound. Observe it and hold it with her.

Ask the wound what it needs. Listen for the answers – they may come in words, images, sounds, or simple knowing. Listen and trust your own intuition, including if your body is asking for rest, food, a good cry, a doctor, a surgeon, a certain food or herb, or lithium from a magic well.

When this feels complete for you, thank Airmed for her witnessing and thank your *awen*, your own inner knowing. Ensure you incorporate this inner listening into the advice of a qualified health practitioner.

JEZEBEL: PRIESTESS OF THE OLD GODS

Jezebel was born in the dark of night during the first storm of the season. Her parents, the priest-king Ithobaal of Tyre and his queen, saw her as a great gift from Baal, the god of lightning and rain who brought fertility to the earth with his life-giving waters. So they named their princess after the ritual cry at the ceremonies that mourned Baal's death before his rebirth: *eze Ba'al* – Jezebel – meaning"Where is the Lord?"

Jezebel grew up surrounded by ceremonies, both royal and religious, immersed in the mysteries and stories of the gods of her people. Baal had defeated the despotic Yam, god of the sea, and took his place as king of the gods. He was a just ruler, working together with the other gods and goddesses. But Mot, the god of death, did not agree that Baal should be king and killed him. This sent Anat, Baal's sister and the goddess of hunting and warfare, into a fury of grief and rage that the people would act out every year. They would dance madly, raking their faces and arms, spilling tears and sometimes their own blood, praying for the return of the flow of rain to feed the crops and people. "She plowed her chest like a garden," they would sing, "she harrowed her back like a valley. She sated herself with weeping. She drank tears like wine."[3] Jezebel would join them in their religious fervor, waiting for the moment when the entire crowd would scream her name passionately: *eze Ba'al, eze Ba'al*, "Where is the Lord?"

Anat's revenge was always Jezebel's favorite part of the story. The fierce goddess put aside her mourning, found the god of death, and cut him into millions of tiny pieces. She winnowed him through a sieve, ground him with millstones, and scattered the pieces of his body across the land to be eaten by birds. This brought Baal back to life, but it was not Mot's end either: the birds who ate Mot's body replanted him as seeds, allowing him a new life.

Jezebel loved all the gods. Astarte, goddess of love and fertility, was so beautiful and elegant that El, father of the gods, would wiggle his toes in anticipation of touching her. Asherah was known as She Who Walks on the Sea, the Mother of all Living. Gula, the great healer, was the guardian of the gates to the Underworld, attended by the dogs that could hurt or heal, depending on what was needed. Jezebel begged her father to be allowed to become a priestess and not have to bother with the work of marriage.

But married she would be. Her father had arranged a diplomatic pairing with Ahab, a faraway king of Samaria, the northern kingdom of Israel. When her father told her this, her face went stony. King Ithobaal looked tenderly at his daughter, understanding her heart. He would miss her dearly, but she was needed for policy, not for the temples. "Remember when Baal was going to kill Yam after their battle, and Asherah and Astarte held him back?"

Jezebel nodded.

"Is Asherah not the queen of the gods? Was Astarte not powerful in guiding the hand of the king, who needed help remembering his role and right action in that moment?"

Jezebel waited. She knew the story well, and her father did too.

"You shall be a queen like that, my little Jezebel. You shall become as powerful to your husband as Asherah is to El. You shall be a priestess. But you must do it as a queen."

Jezebel bit her lip, feeling a quiver of truth in her belly. Besides, she'd been told this King Ahab had already built a temple to Astarte for her near the palace. So Jezebel agreed to travel far from her kingdom by the sea to a dry dusty hill far inland and become the Queen of Israel.

Ahab was strange and dark, his tough skin covered in scars from fighting many battles. But he was kind enough, and intelligent, and his temple to Astarte was perfect, as beautiful and elegant as the goddess herself, an oasis of beauty in a parched and drab town. Jezebel thought they would get along just fine.

And they did. Jezebel often thought of Astarte and Asherah when consulting with Ahab on political issues. When Ahab's army defeated Ben-Hadad, the king of Damascus, she suggested mercy and trade rather than murder and destruction. When the generals arrived in sackcloth, ropes around their necks, and begged for the life of their king, Ahab said simply,

"What, he is still alive? He is my brother. Go bring him to me."

Jezebel smiled as the generals looked at the king in shock. This was to be a kingdom of peace and allyship, not senseless violence.

"It is not the man who puts on armor that should boast," Jezebel offered, "but the one who takes it off."[4] Jezebel had brought Astarte and Asherah's wisdom to Samaria indeed.

Most of Samaria was curious about Jezebel's gods or already worshiped them. But a small group was resentful of her and protective over their god, who went by the name Yahweh, as he was jealous and wanted to rule alone. Jezebel was surprised to find these radicals horrified that Ahab had not murdered Ben-Hadad and everyone from Damascus, taking his wives and children for himself, as was, apparently, the custom. They felt Ahab's mercy was sacrilegious, an indication that the hand of another god (or goddess, in this case) was threatening.

Despite her attempts to keep them in check, this group of radicals grew and swelled from time to time. One of them was a prophet known as Elijah. He was a strange, wild man who lived in the forest, dressed in animal skins, his teeth stained with the fruit of the honey locust tree. He would come out from time to time stinking of sweat and fervor, his hair and beard matted, claiming he had direct access to this god Yahweh, that, oddly, he could ask this god to act for him. He warned of punishment to anyone who turned away from Yahweh and worshiped Jezebel's gods.

Elijah unnerved Jezebel, but she ignored him, for the most part, even when he prophesied that Ahab's blood would be licked by dogs at his death, and that Jezebel would be eaten by dogs at hers. She believed that the majority of the people were behind her and Ahab, that they wanted a peaceful, prosperous kingdom where they could worship whichever gods spoke to their hearts. But she wished Elijah would go away.

Elijah would not go away.

One day he presented the king and queen with a challenge. The region had been plagued by drought the last three years, which was not uncommon. But Elijah claimed he could bring back the life-giving rains himself on behalf of Yahweh. Two sacrifices, he told them, one to Yahweh and one to Baal, must be offered on Mount Carmel. Only one would light, proving the one true God.

"One true God?" Jezebel asked Ahab. "There are many gods, and goddesses too. What is the meaning of this, declaring one true and the others, what, false?"

Ahab sighed. "Yahweh is the one true God for my people. He commanded us to worship him alone."

"But the gods do not do as we ask them to do. They do as they wish, as it pleases them. Humans cannot control the gods, and acting as if we can would be a sacrilege. Is this not true with your Yahweh as well?"

Ahab thought for a moment. "Yahweh has always promised to help and protect the people. He does not wish to work with the other gods, but works with his chosen people. I know it must be hard to understand, my love, but we must believe our God can intercede for us. Otherwise we would have perished long ago. We must accept this challenge."

"The rains must come eventually," Jezebel said, partly to herself. "Perhaps this madman has some sense of the rolling clouds in the distance, some quiver of moisture in the air, and wants to make a spectacle in his favor."

"Perhaps." Ahab continued to stroke his dark beard, his eyes far away.

Jezebel thought of Yam and Baal. They had fought over primacy, and Baal had clearly won. Thanks to Astarte and Asherah, Yam survived, and the two gods made peace, simply ruling in their own domains.

"Very well, my love," Jezebel said. "We will meet this challenge. But I shall not attend and neither should you."

So it was that Elijah led a great procession to the peak of Mount Carmel, where his magic trick would be performed. Four hundred and fifty priests of Baal and four hundred priestesses of Astarte attended. Nearly the entire town was there, invested in the great battle of the gods.

Two bulls were sacrificed and prepared, one for Baal and one for Yahweh. Elijah indicated that the Baal priests should go first.

The priests began to perform the mourning ceremony, invoking Anat's grief, calling for Baal's return. They danced and sang, they screamed and raked their faces like her, they cut their skin and let tears and blood flow to the ground, hoping to invite the flow of life-giving rain that Baal's death had taken away from them.

Hours went by, and Elijah taunted them. "Perhaps your god is sleeping, or pissing against a wall," he laughed as the priests chanted and sorrowed in their exhaustion. At last their humiliation was over, their sacrifice still unlit. It was Elijah's turn.

Elijah strode up to the sacrifice like a stage magician at his craft. He piled it with stones and insisted on pouring four jars of precious, life-giving water over it, a gesture of confidence and showmanship. Then he knelt and quietly spoke to his god.

Suddenly and unmistakably, the sacrifice alit. It burned powerfully, licking up the water that had been poured on it. A great crash of thunder boomed and thick drops of rain began to fall on Mount Carmel, the people at last released from the drought that had gripped them for three years. Yahweh, along with Elijah, was the clear winner.

Elijah's eyes went wild with victory and righteousness. "Yahweh is your one and only Lord!" He proclaimed to the people. They fell to their knees in relief and gratitude, their faces pressed to the wet dirt. "Take hold of the priests of Baal and priestesses of Astarte," Elijah instructed them. "Do not let a single one escape. Do this in the name of your true God, Yahweh."

With these chilling words and a people hypnotized, they took all four hundred and fifty priests and four hundred priestesses down the side of the mountain. Together with Elijah, they murdered every single one of them.

Elijah, splattered with blood and ash, filled with the fury of devotion and bloodthirst, ran all the way down the hill to Jezebel's palace, where he found her standing on her balcony. She stood still, her arms raised to the heavens, feeling the rain soaking her hair, her face, and her gold-threaded robe, the deep royal purple invented in her hometown of Tyre. She was murmuring a prayer to Anat and Baal, welcoming the god back to the lands, grateful for his life-giving water. When she opened her eyes, she saw Elijah running toward her and felt a chill down her spine.

"It has been proven, harlot of the gods," Elijah shouted up at her. "And a blood sacrifice has been paid. All your priests and priestesses are dead, dead in the river!" Elijah laughed, blood running in pale pink rivulets down his white beard and barely covered skin, puddling in the mud below him.

Jezebel stared at him. All her priests and priestesses? To kill a priest was beyond taboo, even if he wasn't *your* priest. To kill hundreds was an insult to all the gods. Elijah had to know what a sacrilege that would be for anyone, of any faith. A deep grief, rage, and bitterness began to brew in her womb.

Jezebel fixed her eyes on the man laughing below her and raised her hands to the heavens again, resuming the posture of prayer and supplication. Bedecked in deep purple and gold, soaked in life-giving rain, she looked every bit the priestess she was. Elijah stopped laughing.

As Jezebel began to speak, two lightning bolts appeared behind her, crossing streams as if they were two heavenly swords clanging together in a mighty battle. "So may the gods do to me, and more also, if I do not take your life for theirs by this time tomorrow. You are Elijah," she proclaimed. "But I am Jezebel."[5] Thunder resounded, seeming to amplify her words. If Elijah could end a drought on his god's behalf, he was about to find out what Queen Jezebel, priestess of Anat, could do on behalf of hers.

Elijah turned and ran for his life.

Jezebel never saw Elijah again, but he had left a shadow on her kingdom as well as on her marriage. Jezebel and Ahab ruled peacefully for many years, despite the growing power of the radicals. Every now and then she heard the rumors they were spreading about her: that she was a harlot, a murderer, even a priest-killer. This made her laugh bitterly – Elijah had been the priest-killer, and Jezebel had spared *his* life.

Ahab seemed troubled, grappling with the part of him that wanted to do right by his god, Yahweh, and the part of him that wanted to be a just king for all his people, whatever they believed. He never strayed from his faith, but never asked Jezebel to stray from hers. Every now and then she would find him laying in his chambers, resting but not asleep, refusing to eat, his brow as white as meadowsweet.

Ahab's life ended at last in battle against the son of his old ally, Ben-Hadad. An arrow had pierced his side, and he staunched it with his robe, insisting on continuing to lead his people from his chariot until his kingdom's victory was assured. Afterward, the radicals insisted Elijah's prophecy had come true, that dogs had licked the blood-soaked chariot when the battle was over.

The mourning Jezebel ruled as Queen Mother as powerfully as she could, doing her best to keep Ahab's lineage on the throne. But Elijah's successor, an even crueler and more powerful prophet named Elisha, had begun his machinations in the nations surrounding Israel and sowed the discontent that would be the downfall of Jezebel's kingdom.

Elisha's preferred weapon was the ambition of the generals and advisors to the kings. He would whisper into their ears, convincing them to murder their kings and take the throne as long as they did Elisha's bidding.

So it did not surprise Jezebel as much as it could have when her son King Joram's general, Jehu, betrayed and murdered him and her grandson, as well, who was by this time the king of Judah. Jezebel knew she was next. She had worked in the name of Baal, Astarte, Asherah, Anat, and El, working towards a peaceful kingdom as prosperous as her homeland in Phoenicia. But these people did not want that. They did not want her. It was time to go with the gods.

As she waited for Jehu to return to the palace for her life, Jezebel asked her attendants to prepare her body. They painted her face with white powder and rimmed her eyes with kohl. They drew delicate lines of henna on her hands and face, including a lotus flower, symbol of Astarte, on her forehead to rest below her most elaborate crown. They adorned her with jewels and gold, her dress the deep royal purple crafted from a humble Phoenician sea snail. They pushed her throne out to her balcony so that she could see Jehu coming, framed in the window like the priestesses of her goddesses often were. Jezebel would not die cowering in the palace. She would die as the Queen Priestess she was, mortal embodiment of the Goddess, and Jehu would understand that in killing her, he was killing the Goddess. And he would face the consequences.

When Jehu arrived, his face streaked with dust, sweat, and blood, he saw the queen, framed in the window, unnervingly beautiful, her head held high, waiting for him. He wavered, speechless.

"Is it peace, traitor, your master's murderer?"[6] Jezebel asked calmly. Wild dogs had begun to circle by his chariot. They whined and barked, feeling the tension in the air.

"Who is with me? Who?" Jehu's voice cracked slightly, trying to suppress his doubt in what Elisha had promised in the name of Yahweh.

Jezebel smirked, knowing Jehu needed someone else to do the deed for him.

Three eunuchs appeared from inside the palace, answering his call.

“Throw her down,” he commanded, trying to find strength and faith in his battle-weary voice.

Jezebel did not resist as the eunuchs pushed her off the balcony. The queen fell to the earth, her blood spattering Jehu’s face and carriage, sending the dogs into a frenzy.

True to Elijah’s prophecy, Jezebel’s body was torn apart by the dogs, eaten and scattered throughout the land, just as Mot’s body had once been by Anat. Like Mot, Jezebel’s essence would be sown widely, seeds to be planted by the wild dogs, the attendants to Gula, goddess of the gates to the Underworld. Thus ended the life and the reign of Queen Priestess Jezebel of Israel. But her legend had only just begun.

JEZEBEL: HARLOT QUEEN

Jezebel was a real person, a princess of Tyre who became the queen of Samaria, her death recorded circa 843 BCE. Even today, her reputation is so powerful that her very name has become a slur synonymous with "traitor" and "harlot." Even the character of Barbie was accused of being a Jezebel in the 2023 Mattel movie *Barbie*.

Jezebel's story, which is detailed in the Biblical books of Kings, is something of a historical fiction, written by her detractors centuries after her death. And yet, even in reading it directly in Kings, it's hard to see Jezebel as quite the villain of her reputation. There are hints that she may have killed or exiled a priest or two, but it's quite explicit that Elijah gleefully murdered hundreds of her priests and (probably) priestesses after his mountain contest was won.

In one particularly chilling story (2 Kings 2:23-25), Elijah's successor Elisha is minding his own business when a group of 42 boys taunt him for being bald-headed – an insult, to be sure, in an era when warriors showed their virility with long, Samson-like hair. But how does our prophet "hero" respond? He conjures two bears to tear apart all 42 children.

Ironically, the plans of Elijah, Elisha, and Jehu go quite horribly wrong after their triumph against Jezebel and the House of Ahab. Immediately after Jezebel's death, Jehu orders the swift beheading of anyone who was related in any way to Ahab's family as well as anyone who dared worship any god but Yahweh. Many of these worshipers were gathered in Jezebel's beloved temple to Astarte, murdered there, and the temple was turned into a latrine. Athaliah, Jezebel's daughter, by now the queen of Judea, went into an Anat-like wrath after this and massacred anyone who appeared to be on the side of Jehu's totalitarian regime. Israel became isolated and vulnerable, leading to a long period of displacement and exile, mostly in Babylon. In her book *Jezebel, the Untold Story of the Bible's Harlot Queen*, Lesley Hazleton writes, "In a stunning example of self-fulfilling prophecy, Elijah and Elisha had helped bring about exactly what they most feared."

Jezebel's story was written in exile by a people who had been traumatized. The writers held that they were being punished for worshiping the wrong gods, and if they could just get back on track, their god would help them again. At the time, gods and goddesses tended to be linked to a specific place, and were often preferred to the other gods in that place. These writers essentially invented the idea of a god that could travel with them into exile, following his people like Oshun did for hers.

Ironically, while Jezebel's tale was written to denounce her and her belief in other gods, the story holds motifs that we've heard before, especially in the legends of Egypt's Isis and Osiris, the Celtic Airmed and Miach, and even the Baal cycle itself, from which we learn about Jezebel's gods.

Like the Canaanite Mot, the Egyptian Set, and the Celtic Miach, Elijah challenges Jezebel. He wins, and her body, like Mot's, Osiris', and Miach's, is scattered across the land and planted as seeds, creating the possibility for a new life in a new form. Jezebel doesn't exactly come back to life, but her reputation has survived to this day, and it is in part through her that we know anything at all about the Canaanite pantheon of gods and goddesses.

In a sense, Jezebel's death was also the true beginning for Yahweh. Monotheism took a few more centuries to fully take hold, but eventually it won out, and Jezebel's tale became a key part of a people's legendary history. How interesting that the ancient tales of agriculture and the secrets of the cycles of death and rebirth should be told here, hidden inside the story of the notorious harlot queen Jezebel.

WORKING WITH JEZEBEL

This ancient story feels eerily resonant with some of the religious politics of the modern day. There are plenty of modern Jezebels asking us to respect each other's beliefs and religions, to remember the old ways while also allowing new ways to come through. And there is no shortage of Elijahs telling us there is just one way we must go, and that if we stray from that path, we risk the wrath of God. Battles over the sacredness of land and worship have barely changed since Jezebel's time, and literal wars are still waged over territory and religious beliefs.

A modern Jezebel is one who insists on remembering the old stories, seeing the patterns between them, and believing in the value of sacred diversity and the history behind political "truths." She is brave, and like so many of the other divine feminine figures in this book, she stays true to herself no matter what other people tell her is true about herself. She doesn't care what people say about her, she knows her own heart. She's me – and maybe she's you, too.

MEDITATION WITH JEZEBEL:

Harlot of the Gods

In this meditation, we will remember Jezebel as a priestess, honoring many gods and goddesses that hold the energies of the natural world within them.

Consider the land that you are on, your relationship to this land, and the lands of your ancestors. Consider the god or gods that live on this land and within your family tradition. Then remember Jezebel's land, the sea island of Tyre, now inland in Lebanon, and the dry northern regions of ancient Israel, and the many gods that once lived there together.

Set a circle of protection, ensuring that only energies that are in alignment with the highest good may enter here. Then invite whatever gods or goddesses you've learned about, the ones in your family's tradition, your country's tradition, or the ones that resonate with you, wherever you may be from. Imagine yourself surrounded by these divine figures, each powerful in their own right, with their own elements to express and their own lessons to teach. Each represents elements of the natural world, like winds, storms, fire, water, healing, even dogs. Feel all these energies around you and within you, the polyphony of divine energy that is always present, if not always named. They may feel completely separate to you, or they may all connect to one single divine source.

Consider the season, the weather, the Moon. Consider the beams of wood and steel that keep you safe, the titans of invention that brought many of the powerful technologies around you to life. Consider yourself, a collection of bacteria and DNA, bones and flesh, disparate pieces come together to create a whole. Honor the multiplicity of the divine in everything. It's here with you right now.

Stay with these divine energies as long as feels right for you. Certain deities may come forward with images or messages for you, or you may simply feel them as a layered pantheon. Take as long as you like here.

When you're ready, invite Jezebel into this space with you. See her power and her wisdom, her fierceness, her dignity, the energies of the love goddess Astarte, the mother Asherah, and the warrior goddess Anat within her. Attend to her, asking her questions if you like, but ensure that you listen if she has any wisdom to share.

When this feels complete for you, thank Jezebel and the many gods and goddesses of the world for who they are and all they do. Bow to them and then close your circle.

RHEA SILVIA: VESTAL VIRGIN

Rhea Silvia was named after Rhea, the mother of the Olympian gods, a goddess of the people of her father, King Numitor of Alba Longa. Rhea's husband, Cronus, had swallowed all of her children, fearing a prophecy that one of them would overtake his rule. But Rhea enlisted the help of the goddess Hekate, who showed her how to swaddle a rock and give that to Cronus instead, thus saving the infant Zeus. This youngest child, the storm god, the lightning bearer, did indeed overthrow Cronus and became King of the Gods.

But Rhea Silvia was also named after Silvia, goddess of the forest of her mother's people, the ancient people of the mountains, here long before the city of Alba Longa. Silvia was the spirit of the trees, the birds, and the wild animals of the forest. As she was growing up, the princess would follow her mother into the mountain woods, finding Silvia in the morning dew, the flash of a hunting fox, and the medicines of the beech trees and rock jasmines that enriched the forest floor.

The princess especially loved the banks of the blond Tiber River, the sweet, fresh, flowing waters that she would wade into up to her waist, singing the songs of her mother's people, feeling the gentle flow of the water caress her body. She would return to the palace covered in mud, her hair scented with spruce needles, her fingers stained with the juice of figs foraged by the Tiber.

Once bathed and dressed, Rhea Silvia would sit by the fire, the abode of the goddess Vesta. This goddess of the hearth held the warm safety of civilization, of the family unit, the energies that keep the wild at bay. The girl would stare into the flames, wondering about this domestic goddess, her heat and power, her centrality in every home in Alba Longa. Sometimes she would stare so long she would see things, strange things, things she didn't understand. She would see her mother fleeing into the forest, her uncle's face, cold and angry, her brothers lost. Sometimes she would see a donkey, the sacred animal of Vesta, who once brayed at just the right moment, warning the goddess of danger and protecting her from rape.

One day, Rhea Silvia was lost in the dance of the forest, playing in the Tiber, drinking its sweet waters, raining its cool water over her naked skin, reveling in its beauty and power. She began to sing in a language she didn't know, a strange sound that felt sweet and delicious in her throat. She closed her eyes and opened her hands to the heavens, feeling the streams of water lick pleasurably down her body, her throat open and resonant.

But when she opened her eyes, she startled: she was surrounded by a pack of wolves, all howling, calling out along with her song. The wolves quieted, looking at her with their intelligent amber eyes. Rhea stood with them in reverent silence for a long moment until, all at once, the pack turned away and disappeared into the forest.

That night, she stared into Vesta's fire. She could still feel the wolves' eyes on her, still sense their friendship, their deep knowing. She asked Vesta with her heart what it meant, and to her surprise, the fire told her. The dreamlike images she had seen in bits and pieces before began to come together. Her uncle Amulius was planning to depose her father and kill her brothers and herself. But she had a choice: the goddess would protect her if she avowed herself as her priestess, a Vestal Virgin.

Rhea stood, horrified. The Vestals were cold and intimidating, different from everyone else in the city. They gave thirty years of their lives to chastity. If she agreed – on pain of death – Rhea would be an old woman before she could experience making love.

But it wasn't long before Rhea understood that Vesta was giving her her one and only chance to live. As the fire had predicted, her uncle came for her and her family in the dark of night, killing her brothers with a single slice of his sword, then turning his murderous eye upon her. But she stood her ground, howling with rage at what he had done. The sound of her keening filled the darkness around the castle, mixing with that of her mother's, who was kneeling over her sons' lifeless bodies. Suddenly, dozens of sharp amber eyes filled the once quiet room, now stained with blood, and fixed on Amulius. Two she-wolves moved between him and Rhea Silvia, snarling. Rhea would not be fighting alone.

Amulius' niece looked much older than her fourteen years. She could have been a queen, a goddess of the wolves. "So may the gods do to you as you have done to my family," Rhea spoke, her voice resonant and clear, a flame in her eyes. "You are Amulius, but I am Rhea Silvia, avowed to the goddess Vesta. Touch me and face the consequences."

Amulius froze, then sheathed his sword, resisting the odd urge to bow to this commanding woman. He knew the consequences of harming a priestess of Vesta, and her vow of chastity would protect him from any future heirs to challenge his position. He mustered up his strength and his voice. "Very well, niece," he spoke. "I will leave you alive as long as you are a virgin of Vesta. But the throne is mine." His eyes darted to the wolves as he spoke, betraying his fear. Rhea did not speak, but held steady, the fire of the goddess in her eyes. Amulius backed away, disappearing out of the castle. The wolves followed slowly, snarling and barking, but let him go.

When he was out of sight, Rhea at last collapsed to her knees, spreading her body over her brothers with her mother. Numitor stared out into the darkness, incomprehensible loss and shame in his eyes.

The former king and queen took refuge in the mountains, nursing their grief and rage with Silvia's people. True to her word, Rhea set out for the city the next day, and devoted her life to the service of Vesta.

It wasn't a bad life. Rhea tended the fire and learned from her sisters, who were kind and confident, not nearly as intimidating as they had seemed before she was one of them. She liked the power the Vestals had, even in their servitude. She also found she had more freedom than she expected to visit her beloved wild wood and spend time in the Tiber River. She found a grove laced with willows, their long branches dipping into the clear water. It was quiet there, and clean, and she would dance with the river god Tiberinus. Sometimes she would call the wolves with her song. She learned about their quiet gentleness, their fierceness, and their cleverness in hunting and foraging.

But Rhea missed her family. She was sometimes overwhelmed by her rage at what Amulius had done. She would fantasize about what she would do to him if they met again. She discovered that she could speak her curses powerfully enough over a pile of dry wood that it would ignite, giving her flame to warm her hands on the cold nights. She would speak them like spells into the river, tell them to the wolves, and scream them into the sky, her body open to the Sun and clouds, thinking of murder and revenge.

One day, murmuring quietly to herself, ruminating on her rage, she heard a voice calling her name. She stood, startled, rushing to cover her naked skin.

There stood a beautiful young man, barely clothed himself, nothing but an animal skin to cover his groin. "Are you looking for these?" He tenderly lifted her white vestments from the crook of a nearby sycamore and handed them to her, barely able to turn his eyes away. Rhea dressed herself quickly.

"I heard your prayers," the strange man said. His eyes were the color of obsidian, the light of faraway battlefields in his eyes, his cheekbones high and dark. He looked familiar.

"My prayers?" Rhea asked.

"Your prayers for justice, to right the wrongs that have been done to you. Your grief and rage rend my heart. I have come to help." The man's image flashed, suddenly, to a soldier in battle, a great spear in his hand, a helmet with a giant fan on his head.

"Mars?" Rhea whispered incredulously. The god of justice and warfare only smiled.

She had connected with the gods and goddesses before, but only in flashes, never something this real, this tangible. Mars smiled gently, offering his hand as one would to a frightened deer.

She looked at him, watching his face for any sign of a prank, a sudden move, the shimmering of a fever dream. When she touched his hand, it was warm and soft, alive and real. He gently held her hand in return, and she could feel him resisting his desire to pull her closer. He reminded her of one of her wolves, and she remembered that the animal was sacred to this god.

"Someone has done you wrong. Done wrong to your family, but also to this forest, to the land, to the people."

Rhea nodded.

"You are powerful. You shine brighter than the other mortals. You are a favorite of Silvia and Tiberinus, and of course Vesta. I wanted to meet you in person." Rhea startled. Even though she was now Vesta's, she would never not be Silvia's, her namesake, or Tiberinus', the god of her beloved river.

"We could help you. Together."

"Together?" Rhea was confused by how she felt around this beautiful man, with his reputation for valor and violence but also, ultimately, peace. Mars fought willingly, but always for justice, often to protect the land, especially the forest.

"If you wish, beautiful human." He leaned in as if to kiss her forehead, but stopped himself. "I will see you again."

With that, the god disappeared as suddenly as he had come. Rhea lifted her fingers to her face, the feeling of his warmth still lingering there.

When Rhea returned to her duties at the temple, she was distracted, thinking about her encounter with the god. She was lost in reverie while attending the temple fire one evening, staring into its flames. An image appeared in the fire. The phallus, the sacred object, taking the form of a tall obsidian rock, smooth and shining even within the smoke and flames. A sister behind her gasped.

"The *fascinus*," Fabia exclaimed. "Vesta wants a child!"

Rhea, shocked, tore her gaze away from the fire. "You can see it, too?" she asked. Fabia nodded.

Fabia gathered the others, asking each of the Vestals to look into the flame to confirm what they were seeing. All nodded.

The oldest, Isabella, spoke. "I have only heard of it in legends," she said. "But its meaning is clear. A child is to be born by one of us. Who saw it first?"

Fabia looked at Rhea Silvia.

"It is a great honor," Chief Vestal Lucina spoke, looking at Rhea. "But make no mistake – this is not a time to break your vows. The child will come through the gods. Be very careful, sisters," she warned. "Trust that Vesta will find her way."

Fabia looked down. A cold silence fell over the sisters. All knew they would be buried alive if they broke their vows, even if they were raped. Rhea knew it had happened, but it was so rare that anyone would bother a sister, and even rarer that a sister dared break her vows. Everyone in this room was now at risk.

"Speak of this to no one," the chief Vestal told them quietly. "Go on. Return to your duties." They did so solemnly, Rhea barely able to control the tremor in her hands.

As soon as she could get away, she rushed back to the grove. Mars was waiting for her, cooling his feet in the gentle waters of the Tiber.

"Good afternoon, Rhea Silvia," he said to her, his smile inviting and gentle, her name clear and resonant in his mouth. "Would you like to sit next to me?" He offered, gesturing to a comfortable place beside him on the sun-warmed rock by the river. He had placed a light white blanket over the rock to make it more comfortable of them both.

Rhea sat, removing her sandals, and joined Mars in cooling her feet in the sweet waters. She could feel the god's warmth next to her, and found the desire to touch him almost overwhelming. But she did not.

"Did you see my gift for you in the fire, Rhea?" He asked.

"Your gift? The... fascinus?"

"I have been conversing with Vesta. She agrees that a wrong has been done to your family, to the land, and that it must be corrected. We are in accord on this matter."

Rhea gaped.

"She had a plan for you long before I heard your prayers, actually," the god continued. "She took you in to protect you from your uncle, but you were always meant to produce heirs. Your children will grow to be great, renowned all over the world."

Rhea tensed. "I was told that the fascinus means Vesta wants one of us to provide her with a child," she told him, flicking her feet in the water.

"Not all wars are fought in battle," Mars told her. "Some are fought in love." He caught her gaze, the dark pools of his eyes endless. She had always thought the god of war would be terrifying, cold, and cruel. But he felt warm and wise, more like a protector than someone to fear. Rhea felt her body leaning closer to him, her lips tingling at the anticipation of his touch. He waited patiently, his passion palpable, but his body still. Rhea pulled away.

"I have made a vow of chastity," she told him softly. "If I were to break these vows, even for a god, I could be killed. Especially if I were to become pregnant."

"I know the mortals' rules," Mars offered. "If we come together today, we plant seeds for a future that this land is destined to see. You would become pregnant. Vesta, Tiberinus, and I will continue to protect you. There are bigger things than your vows at play here, my Rhea. But you must be willing. You must be courageous. I will not force you."

It was all Rhea needed to hear. She leaned into her desire, pressing her lips to the god's, wrapping her arms delicately around his strong neck, feeling his smooth dark skin. His mouth parted slightly, letting her in, feeling her as she felt him. As the god wrapped his large hands around her ribs, holding her close, touching her in ways no one had before, she felt as if she was dancing in ecstasy in the Tiber River, but with another warm body, with love and intensity, with the power of creating new life and power through love, through touch. As they grew closer, she also felt the spark of rage, war, and revenge under her skin, the power of a woman's body that could not be controlled by men. In her rapture, she felt more powerful than her cruel uncle, more powerful than the death of her brothers, more powerful than herself, somehow.

Afterward, Mars laid his blanket over the soft grass under a sycamore tree and held Rhea, their breath matching and slowing together. They watched the willow branches grazing the calm water as Rhea felt the seeds planted in her belly giving her the strength and courage she associated with her wolves.

The lovers rested by the water in the warm sun for an endless time. At some point, Rhea found herself back in the temple, her clothes pristine, her hair set straight, as if nothing had happened. She wondered again if she had been dreaming, but there was a tingle, a light in her belly, that she knew was real.

As time went on, Rhea discovered that she was indeed pregnant, with twins. As she began to show beneath her robes, the sisters who had been with her in the temple when the fascinus appeared doted on her, feeding her extra bread and sheep's milk, separating pomegranate seeds for her. They would walk in a formation around her, protecting her image from the public. They did not even need to ask what happened to understand that she was carrying the child Vesta had asked for.

Despite her sisters' protection, rumors spread, and the news eventually reached King Amulius. He arrived with great pomp and circumstance, ready to punish whichever of the Vestals had broken their vows. He relished the chance to kill a sacred priestess, a woman with power that threatened his own.

Rhea stepped forward immediately, her belly visibly round. "I did not break my vows, uncle," she said, her eyes unflinching. "The children in my belly belong to Vesta and the god Mars."

Amulius was startled to see his niece, her blue eyes and dark hair much like his own. It had been a long time since they had seen each other, but there was to be no mistake who they were to each other. His eyes flashed to her belly, horror coming over his face as he realized she had, indeed, produced an heir that could challenge his right to the throne. He looked away from her and addressed the crowd. "She is to be executed by live burial, as is the custom!" He proclaimed.

"No!" shouted Fabia, her friend and sister, "these are the children of the god Mars!" The Vestals murmured in agreement, and many reached out to touch her, including the chief Vestal of their temple. The touch of a Vestal could immediately absolve someone accused of a crime. The people saw the Vestals as representations of the gods, and they bowed to Rhea.

Amulius cleared his throat, trying to think of a way to get rid of Rhea's heirs without causing an uprising. "Very well," he spoke at last. "She shall not be executed. She will stay at the palace until she gives birth."

Soldiers immediately surrounded Rhea, who snarled quietly. She could see through her uncle's ruse. But she was in no position to argue at this point, and she hoped this would buy her time to figure out how to save herself and her children.

Sure enough, Amulius locked her in a room and chained her, limiting her movement. She was attended to, fed and watered, but as a prisoner. She was grateful there was a small fire in this room so that she could pray to Vesta for help and rescue, and she did so every night.

When her labor pains began, the fire brightened, and she heard a voice, the beautiful, clear tones of Vesta herself. "I am with you, my Rhea. You are brave and you must continue to be brave. Trust." Suddenly, Mars was there, invisible to everyone but her, standing sentinel through her birth. He eased the pain of her wrists against her shackles, holding her steady as her contractions rocked her.

At last, two boys were born, healthy and squalling. One was blue-eyed just like Rhea, and the other was dark and intense, looking much like Mars himself. The infants were wrapped in blankets and handed to their mother to hold and to suckle. Mars held Rhea as she held her infants, and Vesta warmed the room, tending to the girl's wounds, building her strength back up quickly, as she would need it for what was to come.

Rhea was allowed to be with her boys for a mere day before Amulius came to collect them, as Vesta and Mars had warned he would. She cried, the desperate wail that she had heard her mother make so many years ago when her brothers were taken by this same man. She heard wolves howling alongside her from the woods outside the castle, feeling their rage and grief growing as hers did.

"Trust," she heard Mars' voice say.

"Trust," Vesta's calm voice repeated.

But days passed, and Rhea was without her children. Her rage consumed her, her heart somewhere outside of her body, buried deep in the cold Alba Longan dirt. She swore she could hear the whispers of wandering ghosts, drawn to her in her grief. She longed to hunt her uncle with the wolves, to tear him apart from the inside out. She could not live without her children.

So Rhea Silvia made an unusual demand.

"I request the living burial," she told the king. His eyes widened in surprise. No one could hurt a Vestal or spill their blood, so the only way to execute them was to bury them alive them underground. But even this was a slow process: she would be given food and light in an underground chamber and left there to die so that no one could be blamed for her death.

"No one requests the living burial," Amulius spoke.

"I cannot live without my children. I have not broken my vows, but you have shamed me as a priestess of Vesta. I cannot live. My blood will be on your hands, one way or another," she spoke, her eyes flashing, a remnant of the girl in the woods surrounded by wolves returned to Amulius' mind.

Amulius was unnerved, but Rhea was giving him a solution to his problem. "Very well," he said hesitantly.

Rhea's attendants prepared her body. They powdered her face and dressed her in her finest ceremonial clothes. Then they placed her in a litter that would move through the city as a funeral procession, taking her to the edge of the city where she would be interred, followed by her sisters and many in the town who saw her as a mother of gods.

When they arrived, the executioner let down a lamp and a small amount of food to the small chamber. Rhea paused before walking down the short steps to look Amulius in the eye.

"Hail the mother of the children of Mars!" shouted someone from the crowd. "Hail Vesta!" It sounded like Fabia. No one was supposed to speak at an event like this, but the crowd murmured in agreement. Forcing Amulius to publicly kill a Vestal chosen by the gods would turn the tides of public opinion against him. Rhea Silvia had found a way to undermine him again. Amulius clenched his jaw and ordered the chamber sealed.

It was very dark in the chamber, and Rhea felt a little fear creep into her stomach. She hoped her plan would work.

She lit the lamp, grateful for the small flame. She stared deeply into it, calling on Vesta and Mars together. As the oxygen burned in the small chamber, Rhea's body flickered as if it, too, was made of the light of Vesta's fire.

And then her body was gone. Nothing remained but the small flame which eventually flickered out.

Rhea Silvia's spirit scattered across the forest. She caressed the sycamore trees as wind. She undulated with the waves in the Tiber River. She entered the wild eyes of the foxes and bears. She found herself in the heart of her favorite mother wolf, seeking the scent of the twins on the air. The wolf found the infants, shivering and crying but safe, on the banks of the Tiber where Amulius' servant had left them, unable to drown them as he'd been instructed. She took them into her den, warmed them with her fur, and suckled them at her breast, making them as strong as her own pups. When it was time, she found a kind farmer and his wife who took the boys into their warm home, naming them Remus and Romulus.

Now a spirit of the forest, Rhea Silvia watched her boys grow, supporting them as the wind and the river, the power of the wolf and the nourishment of the trees. When they came of age, she helped them discover their true identity, and the sons of Mars and Rhea Silvia overthrew Amulius, reinstated Numitor, and went on to found the great city of Rome. Rhea Silvia, Vestal Virgin, daughter of Alba Longa, spirit of the forest, at last had claimed her revenge.

RHEA SILVIA: MOTHER OF ROME

The founding of Rome is a story that likely involves some combination of folklore, mythology, and history. While Rome was founded around 750 BCE, this tale wasn't seen in writing until around the third century BCE. In some versions, Rhea Silvia was in love with Mars, while others say the god (or someone else) raped her.

As common as it was for a god to rape a mortal, the Roman Mars wasn't quite as intensely difficult as his Greek counterpart, Ares. Mars was a god of war, but he was also a guardian of the land and agriculture. One of his forms was *Mars Silvanus*, Mars of the Woods. His warfare was usually waged in the interest of peace and protection.

The goddess Vesta was generally worshiped in the form of a flame. She was a virgin goddess, but she was also a fertility goddess, powerful over the hearth and the family home. Her Vestal Virgins had unusual power and position in Roman society. Occasionally, the symbol of the phallus was said to appear in the hearth fire, a magical symbol referred to as the *fascinus* or *fascinum* (which also gives root to our modern English word "fascinate"). The sixth king of Rome, Servius Tullius, claimed to have been conceived this way, between a Vestal and the god Vulcan.

In some stories Rhea Silvia is drowned in the river, perhaps to become the divine wife of the river god Tiberinus. Sometimes she throws herself into the river, sometimes she is buried alive, and in some stories, Amulius' daughter Antho (or a servant) finds a way to spare her life. Whatever may have really happened, Rhea Silvia's legacy remained, known to this day as the mother of Rome.

WORKING WITH RHEA SILVIA: VESTAL VIRGIN

Rhea Silvia was a princess, a priestess, and an avowed virgin, the victim or the lover of Mars. But perhaps she was also something of a Jezebel, a woman who found her way to power and justice through divine intervention. Maybe she was also a witch, connected to the powers of the forest through her mother and the old ways that were there before the patriarchal gods of Rome took power.

As a Vestal Virgin, Rhea Silvia held a position of feminine power in a world that tended to privilege men. She resists not only by taking this role, but by performing one of the most ancient powers that only people with wombs can perform: giving birth. Her act of creating life disrupted all that King Amulius was trying to control with violence. Like Jezebel, Rhea Silvia wasn't able to maintain a world where the ancient feminine powers of the Goddess were supreme. But her story and her essence was scattered throughout the land, remaining there forever, even if only as legend.

MEDITATION WITH RHEA SILVIA:

The Powers of the Wildwood

If you have access to a forest or wooded region, you could try doing this meditation while walking or sitting in that natural landscape. If not, simply explore it with your imagination. Consider the land that you are on right now, the wildwoods of this region. Consider Rhea Silvia's land, the long-lost Alba Longa, the forests of ancient Italy.

Take a deep breath, filling your lungs with the scent of the woods. What can you detect or imagine in that smell? What trees, what dirt, what indications of the season? Observe the world with your eyes (or inner eye). What colors and textures can you see? What plants and maybe animals are present with you in this beautiful place? What sounds can you hear? What does the wind feel like in the trees? Are there rustles, croaks, birdcalls, other music of the woods? If you listen very closely, can you feel the underground mycelium connecting and communicating?

Allow your thoughts to quiet and tune in to the ancient wisdom of the wildwood, the ecosystems that cycle daily and yearly without the need of any human intervention. Feel the presence of death, life, and possibility all at once.

When you're ready, invite Rhea Silvia to join you here. She comes with all the pain and power of her human existence as well as her magic as a legend, as a spirit of the forest and the river. You may have questions for her, she may have messages for you, or you may simply sit together, being with each other in this beautiful place. When you're ready, thank Rhea Silvia deeply for her wisdom and presence. Thank the wildness of the woods, the knowing of the ecological world, of the land that you are on.

MATANGI: THE OUT-CASTE GODDESS

Once upon a time, the great goddess Parvati and her consort Shiva were making love in the cremation grounds, as was their custom. When they were finished, they held each other, and Parvati noticed her body smeared with dark ash.

"My love, why do we always make love here? Why not in a beautiful home, on clean, jasmine-scented sheets?"

"My bliss," Shiva replied, drawing a lotus flower on her forehead with the ash from his finger, "we do not need jasmine scented sheets. The divine is everywhere, in everything, in the fingernails of a corpse, in the ashes from the cremation grounds, even in the sacred work of the Chandala, the lowest caste of society."

Parvati's brow furrowed. Her normally creamy brown complexion flashed black, her eyes a bloodthirsty red, her teeth suddenly growing fangs. "You do not need to teach me what I have taught you!" she growled. "Do you not think I understand the sacredness of the everything, which is all that I am?"

Startled, Shiva placed a hand on his divine wife's arm. "Of course I do, my joy. Calm yourself." He leaned in to try to kiss her again, but she turned away.

"I'd like to go visit my father in the mountains," she said abruptly, her face returning to normal.

"Your human father? Why, my love? Please don't go. Stay here and teach me, make love to me. Do not run away." He lay back in the pile of ash, reveling in the soot and char that was once a human being.

"I wish to leave," Parvati told him, rising and covering herself with a lush red robe.

Shiva knew better than to argue with his wife, the goddess that presided over everything in the universe, including, essentially, himself. She always went to the mountains when she was annoyed with him. "Fine," he sighed. "But do not stay long or I will come looking for you."

"Fine," she said, and hooked her fingers around the claw of a great crane that had appeared at her command, ready to carry her to the mountains.

Parvati did not return in a few days. She was indeed annoyed with Shiva, who had doubted that she valued the low, the outcast, the ugly, as much as he did. She simply wanted to make love in a jasmine-scented bed once in a while. She knew her beloved well, however, and wasn't surprised when Shiva showed up in the mountains. The great god appeared at Himavat's palace as a humble ornament seller. He offered Parvati conch shell earrings, shaped exactly to her preference. She accepted them and asked the cost. "A night of love with me," the seller told her.

Parvati raised an eyebrow. She had no trouble seeing through Shiva's disguise, and if he meant to test her loyalty, she had already won the ruse.

"All right," she smiled softly, to Shiva's surprise. "But not just now. I'll find you later," she told him, and closed the door in his face.

Giggling a little to herself, Parvati immediately transported back to Shiva's dwelling, where he was in meditation, projecting his body into the Himalayas. Parvati took on a disguise of her own: a Chandala woman, a huntress of the forest, an out-caste, untouchable by someone of higher rank. She was beautiful, a sixteen-year-old woman, her full breasts smeared with red kumkum powder. Her ornaments and clothing were rich blood red, and around her neck was a garland of poisonous gunja berries from the forest. A crescent Moon adorned her forehead like a crown. Her clothing was nothing but leaves, and she wore the beautiful conch shell earrings Shiva had sold to her as the ornament seller. She represented everything someone of position was not supposed to touch.

She danced seductively in this form, her wide hips rolling, her delicate arms moving in elegant arcs, her jewels gently tinkling as she moved her body. The parrots chattered and sang along with her rhythm. She began to perspire lightly, which made her all the more alluring.

Shiva became aware of this beautiful Chandala woman dancing near his dwelling, and rose from his meditation to see what was happening. He was entranced by her beauty and sensuality, charmed by something familiar about her he couldn't quite put his finger on.

"Who are you?" he asked the woman.

"I am Prakriti," she told him, "the daughter of a Chandala, a huntress of the Savara tribe. I am here to do penance." She approached him, her wide eyes meeting his, the sweat dewy on her chest.

"I am the one who provides fruits for those who do penance," he told her, taking her hand and drawing her to him. As he stared into her depthless eyes, he recognized what was so familiar – it was his own wife, Parvati, returned to him in the play of love. He embraced her, and as their lips met, Shiva himself turned into a Chandala, an outcast, a wild man of the woods. The two made love passionately, deeply connecting with each other in the form of that which is most distasteful, rejected from society, seen as unclean and improper.

When the two were fully satisfied and completely polluted by each other, they changed back into their original forms, resting on the forest floor, watching the parrots float above them, singing songs of love.

"Now that we are both Chandala," Parvati told her husband, "do you understand that I revere and honor the rejected?"

"Of course I do, my love, I have always known that. Otherwise why would you have accepted me?" Shiva laughed, gesturing to his blue, ash-smeared skin, his long dreadlocks, and his tendencies to prefer the outskirts of polite society.

Parvati kissed her husband's ashy skin, pressing some of her kumkum powder into his chest.

"From now on I shall be revered as the goddess Ucchista-Chandalini, Matangi, goddess of uneaten food, of sweat and dirt and pollution. I will be offered leftovers, food that has been tasted or dropped on the floor by unwashed hands and unclean bodies. And I will give great boons to anyone who worships me in this way."

Shiva, awed by his wife once again, could not have been more pleased. He drank in her outcast lips, her sweaty skin, her polluted breath, and made love to her once again, this time as the goddess Matangi.

MATANGI: POLLUTION, LEFTOVERS, AND OUTCASTS

Matangi is one of the Ten Great Wisdom Goddesses, the *Dasa Mahavidyas*, which are 10 emanations of the divine feminine principle in Hindu Tantra. Shakti, the great goddess, goes by many names, including Parvati and Sati. Shakti's consort is Shiva, the Lord of Destruction, part of the Hindu triplicate of gods including Brahma the Creator and Vishnu the Sustainer.

In one story, Sati gets angry at Shiva, and the Ten Great Wisdom Goddesses appear from within her, surrounding and terrifying him, ensuring she gets her way. In another, the goddess of desire, Tripura Sundari, needs to fight a demon that can only be defeated by a woman. She paints her nails a lovely shade of red, and from each of her 10 fingernails appear the Wisdom Goddesses, who surround the demon and burst him into a million pieces.

Tantra is in itself something of an outcast. It developed out of both Buddhism and Hinduism in separate forms beginning around the first century CE, while classical Hinduism dates back to at least 1500 BCE. In some cases, Tantric practices run explicitly counter to many Brahminical Hindu standards, though many people are both mainstream Hindu as well as Tantric in their own (sometimes secret) ways.

Matangi in particular challenges the concept of the traditional caste system, which is a social hierarchy based on birth and other factors. Brahmins are the highest caste of priests and teachers, Kshatriyas are warriors and rulers, Vaishyas are traders and merchants, and Shudras are laborers and artisans. Below all these are the Dalits, the untouchables, those that deal with tasks too polluting to be assigned to those of higher castes.

Chandalas, who deal with corpses, are the lowest of the low, the most polluting entity in the Hindu imagination, existing literally outside the caste system. Some believe they originated in forbidden unions between Brahmins and Shudras. They also have a relationship with the forest-dwellers, the indigenous people of the wildwood, who live physically outside of the cities and towns. Matangi is connected to the forest, and especially the Savara forest tribe. The wisdom of these people is, perhaps, too wild, too uncivilized, to fit into polite society – especially since they may remember ways that are even older than Hinduism.

Matangi is sometimes described with blue skin, which could represent dark skin or possibly the blue of death, the skin of a corpse, like the Norse Underworld goddess, Hel. When Matangi is depicted as green, she is referencing Kali, the fierce destructor goddess, and Green Tara, who is in turn related to Guan Yin. Much like Hekate, Matangi can be propitiated with offerings of leftover food at a crossroads.

TANTRA

One of the fundamental principles of Tantra is the concept of non-rejection. Everything that exists in the universe is a manifestation of the divine. In a strict Hindu culture that has strong taboos against pollution, both physical and social, Tantric non-rejection challenges the adept to experience the divine in everything: in the cremation grounds, in leftover food, in sweat, death, and human waste. Matangi is the representation of all this, literally the out-caste goddess, the goddess who is worshiped as the lowest of the low, the most polluted, the most exiled.

Tantra is a rich (and secret) tradition that is practiced by those initiated by a guru. Sometimes Tantra can look a little like witchcraft, with special rituals and recipes that can be used to cast spells and influence people.

Many people in the West associate it with sexual practices, and while there is a branch of Tantra that explores sexuality as a divine practice, it's far from universal. It's often understood more like a metaphor, similar to the concept of *hieros gamos*, the sacred marriage, the coming together of masculine and feminine to create life that we see in many ancient pre-patriarchal religions.

WORKING WITH MATANGI

In the story, I've conflated a few of Matangi's origin myths and added some details to illuminate not only her outcast (and out-caste) aspects, but also the Shakta Tantric concept that the divine feminine is supreme, even over the divine masculine.[7] I have not been initiated into these traditions, and India is not my land or my culture. And yet there's something about Matangi and her insistence that the ugliest parts of ourselves are ultimately divine that I can't help but relate to.

Matangi teaches the powerful lesson that working with these exiled elements can give us power over ourselves and others, even giving us direct access to the divine. While keeping purity and avoiding pollution are major practices in mainstream Hinduism and many other religions around the world, Tantra turns this on its head, inviting us to honor and remember (maybe even bathe in and make love to) death, disease, uncleanliness, and the state of being outcast, as avenues toward rather than away from the experience of the divine.

Matangi is also literally the out-caste goddess, the goddess for the reviled and ignored. This is a goddess who wants your leftover food, unclean hands, and cremation ash. She's not interested in you if you are too clean or popular. She wants you to dance with her in the wildwood, to forget your civilized tendencies. When you feel like an outcast piece of scrap, hated, alone, or misunderstood, Matangi wants you. Dance with her.

MEDITATION WITH MATANGI:

Honoring What is Outcast within You

In this meditation, let's reclaim our inner outcasts. Let's welcome our exiled inner children, our addicted parts, our ugliness, our unsavory desires, and let them show us the path to the numinous. Keep in mind that acknowledging and engaging with these parts with compassion can be powerful healing, but be sure that any action you take after this meditation is safe for you and everyone around you.

Acknowledge the land you are on. Consider Matangi's lands, the varying climates of India, and especially the tropical forest where the wild, poisonous gunja berries grow.

Close or soften your eyes and contemplate an aspect of yourself that you find distasteful, unpopular, ugly, or unwanted. It could be a physical part of your body, an emotion, a personality trait, whatever resonates for you. As you bring up this part of yourself, give it a shape, a size, an image, whatever it might be. Check to see if it might be a younger part of you, or recall a younger part in some way. See, feel, or hear this part of you.

Witness it fully. Listen to this part. Honor its lessons. Consider why this part is unwanted, unwelcome in your day-to-day life, and what it brings when you sit with it. Observe any emotions, reactions, or judgments that arise.

Now imagine Matangi here with you. See how she approaches the part of you that you see as polluted, unwanted, outcast. Let her witness with you. Stay here as long as you'd like. Thank Matangi for being here with you, outcasts together.

HEL: GODDESS OF THE NORSE UNDERWORLD

Once upon a time, there was a beautiful prince named Baldr. He was the favorite child of Odin and Frigg, the king and queen of Asgard, the heavenly realm of the gods. Frigg would stroke Baldr's soft, blonde hair, wipe his tears with her fingers, and applaud his great feats as he grew into a great warrior. Baldr was so beautiful his very skin glowed, and though his siblings were jealous of the attention he got from Frigg and Odin from time to time, they couldn't help but love him. It didn't help that he was generous, kind, wise, and merciful.

But beautiful Baldr lived with a shadow. He had nightmares.

One night, a beautiful woman appeared to him in his dreams, beckoning him to come to her, to a dark place he knew to be Helheim, the land of the dead. When she turned, half her face was the blue of death, her skin rotted, blood seeping from her mouth. Baldr felt his life force spilling out of his side, and he felt he had no choice but to follow her.

Baldr woke with a sweat, his brow as white as meadowsweet. He ran to his mother, afraid and confused. When he found her, she shared the look of horror on his face, and he discovered she had been dreaming, too. She held her precious son to her.

"Help me to understand, mother, so that I can protect myself and you. What is the meaning of these dreams?"

"The prophecy tells that one day Ragnarok will come, ending Odin's rule and our world as we know it. It begins with your death," Frigg explained, beginning to cry.

Baldr gently wiped his mother's tears as she used to do for him when he was a boy. He had heard the prophecy before.

"What can I do, mother? How can I help?"

"There is nothing you can do, my love," Frigg told him, a look of determination coming over her face. "But there is something that I can do."

Frigg swept from her bedchambers and prepared for her quest. She would travel across the nine realms, wherever she could reach, and secure an oath from every plant, animal, element, and mineral that it would not harm her most cherished son. Being the most beloved goddess of the nine realms, all agreed easily, and she returned to Asgard triumphant, confident that Baldr would be safe.

But one was not so happy to hear that Baldr would be protected. The god Loki, the magician and shapeshifter, knew the prophecy too. His children, the serpent Jormungandr, the wolf Fenrir, and his daughter Hel were to play an important role in Ragnarok and rule whatever existed on the other side. He knew that Baldr needed to die in order to allow these events to take place.

So Loki transformed himself into one of Frigg's handmaidens and asked her questions while he braided her long, golden hair.

"It must have been quite an ordeal to gain promises from all the creatures of the world not to harm Baldr," Loki said as the handmaiden.

"Not such a burden, dear, as the creatures of the nine realms listen to me."

"You are a great queen indeed," Loki simpered. "Was there any creature you did not gain an oath from?"

Frigg thought for a moment. "Well, of course the young mistletoe is too sweet and gentle to ever cause any harm. I suppose I did not ask the mistletoe to promise an oath."

The handmaiden did not answer, and when Frigg turned around, her hair was perfectly plaited and her handmaiden was gone.

In the meantime, Baldr's brothers had taken up the pastime of throwing different objects at his body and watching them glance off, proving his mother's power to protect him. As they played and joked, Baldr rolled his eyes, a little embarrassed. He wanted to use his invulnerability in battle, to fight for what was right, and something about this felt wrong to him. Though his mother had promised no harm could come to him from any of the creatures of the nine realms, his dreams hadn't stopped. He kept thinking about the beautiful woman who beckoned to him in his nighttime visions.

One day Loki showed up to play with the brothers, disguising himself as one of them. He had fashioned a spear from mistletoe branches, and handed it to Hodr, Baldr's blind twin brother whose aim was always true. "Try this," Loki said, jovially.

Hodr threw the spear, and to everyone's shock, it embedded itself in Baldr's side. Red blood seeped from the wound, soaking the ground beneath him. Within minutes, Baldr was dead.

While the gods in Asgard stared in shock, his mother keening over his lifeless body, Baldr found himself in a strange realm. This was Helheim, the dark Underworld. It was dim, like an eternal twilight, but it was also strangely beautiful. The halls were entirely gold, lit by warm torches and decorated with ornately painted runes.

His footsteps echoed as he walked along the hall, finding himself in a mirrored throne room. Seated there, a tall sunstone crown on her head, was the beautiful half-dead woman of his dreams. One side of her face was pink and soft, her eye the blue of glaciers, her lips the rich, light pink of alpine buttercups. As she turned, just as she had in his dream, the rotten, corpse-like half of her face was revealed, her other eye sunken, lips pulled away from her teeth. But rather than feeling horror, Baldr could only experience reverence. This woman held the line between life and death. She was the queen of the Underworld, and Baldr wanted to know her.

"Welcome, Baldr," she said, her voice echoing in this quiet place. "We have been expecting you." She rose, her figure tall and slim, her white silken robes rustling at her feet. She took his hand gently, and walked with him to a giant feasting hall, a table set with fine tableware for dozens, maybe more. Her hand was cold and gentle, and her touch reverberated on Baldr's skin when she let him go.

Baldr sat down at the massive table across from the queen and looked around. It was only the two of them. He noticed her famous dish, called Hunger, and her knife, called Starvation. But the food on the plates was warm and savory: soft fresh bread, buttered generously, and thick cuts of juicy, tender meat.

The queen lifted a delicate glass filled with dark red wine.

Baldr met her gesture, the clink of the glasses echoing throughout the giant empty feast hall.

"You are Hel, queen of Helheim," Baldr said. She nodded, sipping her wine. "Loki's daughter. Sister to Fenrir and Jormungandr. Cast out of Asgard because of the prophecy of Ragnarok."

Hel laughed delicately.

"They say you reign cruelly over a realm of cold and darkness. But this place is beautiful. Is it truly Helheim?"

Hel looked at Baldr over her glass. "Don't believe everything you hear," she said, half a smile on her lips.

Baldr smiled back, hesitantly. His curiosity pushed him to say more. "They also say you were violent and cruel, that you had to be imprisoned here because you threatened the balance of the universe."

"Would you like to know the truth, dear Baldr?" she asked, her fork piercing a morsel of meat.

"Yes please," he said softly, sipping his wine, which was as rich as it was dark, its aromas heady and wooded, a hint of soft leather and sloe-berry.

"I am not imprisoned here," Hel began. "I created this place. I was always meant to preside over death and dying, to provide a home for those who did not die the valiant death of the warriors Odin keeps for his army at Ragnarok."

"Valhalla," Baldr offered, and a shadow cast over his face. He had always expected that would be where he would spend his afterlife, eating boar meat, battling the other warriors, and preparing for the final fight.

"Odin resists death. He fears it, and so he fears me. He wants to be in power forever. But that would prevent the rebirth and renewal of Ragnarok."

“Rebirth and renewal? Ragnarok is the apocalypse, the end of the world. We are all working to prevent it.”

Hel laughed her beautiful pealing laugh again. “That’s what he told you?” She thought for a moment, sipping her wine. “Ragnarok will likely be a great battle, yes. But that is only because some resist its inevitability. Ragnarok is not bad or evil. It is simply the end of Odin’s world, and the beginning of a new one. Were you ever told that you are to be king of this new world?”

Baldr’s eyes widened. He opened his mouth, but no speech came.

“It is not about Ragnarok. It is about what happens after Ragnarok. A new world, more peaceful, more cohesive, cleansed of the violence of Odin’s realm. You are to reign over this earth, bringing kindness and mercy to the nine realms. Or however many realms that world contains.” The queen looked at Baldr, her long eyelashes heavy over her ice blue eye.

“I shall be there too. Odin likes to tell people he sent me away to protect them from me, but that is not within his power. He wants to stop death, which is not possible. It is not my work to take those before their time, only to care for the ones who must pass over.”

She smiled as Baldr took in this information. “Odin does not like to visit me because I am one of the few beings in the nine realms with more power than him.”

“More powerful than Odin? Than the Allfather, who has the second sight and all the knowledge of the universe?”

Hel broke a piece of bread, its steam releasing from its soft body. “It’s always struck me as funny that he seeks knowledge to prevent that which cannot be prevented. I wait for the day the knowledge will teach him that Ragnarok is simply Death, the inevitable, the cycle of decay and renewal that has always been and will always be.” She paused, contemplating. Then she looked at her guest. “You and I will be there together, Baldr. But your father and your brothers will not.”

Baldr paled, his heart heavy. Hel's face turned sad again as she looked into his eyes. "That is not my choice," she added. Baldr looked back, his warm brown eyes connecting with her ice blue gaze, empathy and care shared between them. Something in Baldr resonated deeply with this strangely beautiful woman, her incredible power to stand at the threshold of life and death, a power that even his father had not been able to claim.

Baldr hesitantly reached his hand across the table towards Hel. He left it open on the table, palm up. Hel gently placed her hand in his, and it felt cool and soft, but somehow very much alive. Despite everything he might have expected to feel, Baldr was quite content to be here in Helheim sharing a meal with this fascinating and powerful woman, the goddess of death whom his father had so feared, who had been outcast for her power, who had been so misunderstood. Hel smiled softly, something of the young girl she once was glimmering through her queenly face. Baldr thought he might be in love.

Meanwhile, Asgard was in chaos. Frigg was beside herself with grief and guilt for having forgotten the innocent-seeming mistletoe. Hodr was in a horrified stupor, knowing he must pay for a murder he did not mean to cause. Odin was in a panic, knowing the death of Baldr meant the path to the end of his rule and his life had been set.

Every night, Frigg tossed and turned, unable to sleep, unable to forgive herself for having failed to protect her son, unable to stop seeing his lifeless body every time she closed her eyes. On one of these nights, she gave up the torture of trying to rest and walked to her window, staring out at Asgard. She saw its cold mountains in the distance, the glint of the golden city in the starlight, and the rainbow bridge to Midgard, the land of the humans, just to the west. She knew that Yggdrasil, the World Tree, spun slowly at the center of their universes, connecting them all.

Frigg imagined Niflheim, the ice world, in the cold north, and then, somewhere deep beneath that, Helheim, Hel's realm, where her beloved Baldr was trapped, probably freezing cold and suffering.

Frigg had an idea.

She flew to the hallways and woke everyone in the palace, insisting they meet around the hearth. She looked at her sleepy sons, many with eyes swollen from crying. Hodr looked haunted, as if his eyes had been carved out and replaced with obsidian. If she could save Baldr, perhaps she could also save Hodr from the terrible fate that he was already living, having accidentally killed his twin brother.

"We shall rescue Baldr from Helheim. We must bring him back. I will give Hel anything she wants in return for my son. It is a dangerous mission, but I will give all my love and favor to any of you brave enough to travel to Helheim and retrieve him."

The room was silent for a moment. Then Hermóðr stood. A strong warrior, incredibly brave, and often overlooked by Odin. "I shall go, mother. I will do what needs to be done."

Without another word, Frigg took Hermóðr in her arms and held him close. Odin, who appeared to have aged since Baldr's death, his wrinkles deeper, his skin more grey, shook Hermóðr's hand and led him to the stable, where he would lend his famous horse, the eight-legged Sleipnir who could traverse the bridge between the land of the dead and the land of the living.

By dawn, Hermóðr was on his way.

The boy and the horse traveled for nine nights and nine days without stopping to the far distant ice world of Niflheim. It was quiet and bitingly cold, with only the whistling of the wind to accompany them. From time to time, Hermóðr was sure he heard the whispers of the dead on the wind.

At last, Hermóðr arrived at the throne room. He found the queen, Hel, her robes a rich dark purple, half her face a young beauty, the other half a rotten corpse. To his surprise, Baldr sat next to her as if he were her king, an odd ease between the two of them. It was not what Hermóðr had expected.

He nodded at his brother, and then knelt before Hel, his forehead bowing low to the ground. "Oh great queen of Helheim! I am here to ask for my brother's life in exchange for anything the Allfather Odin and the great Queen Frigg can offer you. The whole world mourns beloved Baldr and our tears will not stop without your help."

Hel was silent for a moment. "Get up, Hermóðr," she told him. He did so and looked at his brother. Baldr offered a strange smile, sad and encouraging at the same time.

"Baldr is meant to be here at my side. He begins the path to Ragnarok, which cannot be stopped. The Norns have woven the threads of fate. I understand your grief and I feel for you. But this is the way of things."

Hermóðr looked at Baldr again, who nodded slightly. He was expecting his brother to beg to be released from the claws of the outcast Hel, not agree that he should stay with her. He tried again.

"All of Asgard is in mourning. Not a creature lives with dry eyes for the loss of Baldr. You can have anything you wish if you only return him to us." He opened his hands and offered Hel Odin's beautiful golden ring, Draupnir, which would drip eight new rings from itself every ninth night. More gifts spilled from his hands.

Hel looked at the gifts, then turned her gaze to Baldr. The two leaned close and spoke too quietly for Hermóðr to hear them. Baldr nodded.

"I have no need for any of those things," she said. "You may return them to Odin. But if it is true what you say, that every creature, living and dead, weeps in mourning for Baldr, then I will return him to the land of the living. His time here may be delayed, but it cannot be held off forever."

Hermóðr bowed again, deeply. It was enough.

When he returned to Asgard with Hel's message, Frigg and Odin sent messengers across the land, ensuring that every creature, living and dead, would weep for Baldr. All but one did so. Loki transformed himself into a troll named Thökk and refused to cry for Baldr. "Let Hel hold what she has," the troll told the messenger.

So it was that Odin and Frigg failed to stop fate or bargain with Death. Baldr stayed in Helheim with its queen until the inevitable events of Ragnarok came to be. Odin's forces fought it desperately, even though they must have known they couldn't win. After the battle, a great flood immersed the land, washing away all the blood, sin, and pain, and then ebbed away. Beneath its waters, a beautiful new land, warm and fertile, had been born. As dawn arose, so did Baldr and Hel. Death had opened a portal to new life once again.

HEL: OUTCAST OF DEATH

Hel is a rather mysterious figure in the Norse legends. In 793 CE, great warriors known as Vikings from the Scandinavian regions began an era of conquering and piracy that extended their realm into Europe, Iceland, Greenland, Russia, Ukraine, and even to North America in what's now known as Newfoundland, Canada. Many settled in Iceland and made it their new home. While the Vikings settled down, the Norse people thrived, and the tales of these strange warlike heathens spread orally across the lands. Most of the stories we have today came from Snorri Sturluson, a Christian historian writing in Iceland in the early 13th century CE – long after the peak of the Norse era.[8] It's hard to know what was adjusted to fit the Christian narrative. Hel may indeed have gifted her name to the Christian Underworld, "Hell" – a word that does not appear in the eary Bible.

As the story goes, Odin cast out Loki's three children born by the giantess Angrboda, whose name means something like "Sorrow-Bringer," due to the prophecy that these children would play a role in Ragnarok. Odin bound Fenrir, the giant wolf who could shoot fire out of his eyes and nose. He threw Jormungandr, a great serpent, into the ocean where he grew so large he wrapped himself around the world, grasping his own tail. And Hel, the last of the three, was outcast to the icy world of Niflheim and granted authority over the dead of the nine realms, which meant, essentially, everyone and everything.

Why bind Fenrir and throw Jormungandr into the ocean while offering an entire kingdom to the third of these children? If Hel is Death herself, then she had more power than Odin from the beginning. Born half dead, she must have represented the bridge between life and death long before she was banished to Helheim. She is the psychopomp, much like Hekate, the figure that helps guide the living across the threshold to the dead when it is their time. Odin could try to banish her, but even the king of the gods could not completely eliminate Death.

WORKING WITH HEL

Hel joins a long tradition of goddesses who preside over the realm of death and all that is rejected. Her partly blue skin and fearsome nature recall the outcast Matangi and the Hindu goddess Kali, who is both a great destroyer and a great mother, the energy that gives as well as takes.

She reminds us of Persephone, the daughter of the goddess of grain and fertility, who was grieved in the above world, but fell in love with the Underworld. She is like Ereshkigal, the misunderstood goddess of the death realm who had great lessons to teach to Inanna, her sister, goddess of fertility and life, in Mesopotamian mythology. Baldr joins Osiris, Miach, Mot, and even Jesus as a figure that must die to create the possibility of rebirth.

When working with Hel, we are invited to consider how we have cast out the concept of death in our own lives. What are we clinging to, like Odin, that might need to die to let us be born again? Do we fear the inevitable transition from life to death? Can we trust that we will be held, cared for in the realm of the dead with all the others who have gone before us?

MEDITATION WITH HEL:

Sitting with Death

If we have outcast death, let's invite it back in. When we fully allow the truth of death and loss, we can stop trying so hard to avoid the inevitable and become fully present with life.

Light your candle and set your circle. Acknowledge the land you are on. Consider Hel's lands, the cold northern regions of the Norse people.

Now consider death. What comes up for you when you think about this concept, whether literal or metaphorical? Notice what is coming up in your body.

Now imagine Hel is with you in this moment. Half her face is beautiful, and half is terrifyingly corpse-like. Witness her, look her in the eyes, and see her gentleness, her beauty, her intention to care for those who pass into her world. She is not here to scare you or even to take you to her realm. When it is your time, she will guide you gently across the worlds, ensuring your safe passage to the land of the dead. What lessons does she have for you here? What wisdom can she teach you if you listen? If you have outcast death, what would it look like to allow it back in, as a healthy and necessary aspect of life?

When this feels complete, thank Hel deeply for being with you.

ASHERAH: THE EXILED GODDESS OF THE BIBLE

Once, We built this world together, He and I. We created light and darkness, water and fire, earth and air. We made human beings in our image, male and female. We created them. We made snow and sand, desert and mountain. We made ice and dirt, and seeds that would grow to be great date palms, providing nourishment for our people.

We had seventy children, He and I. They were beautiful, all our babies, the *Elohim*. Anat was the fierce one, bloodthirsty, ready to fight for justice. Astarte was so beautiful and powerful, able to get what she wanted with nothing more than a look. Yam was my child of the sea, from which everything was born. Mot, our saddest child, took the realm of Death. Then there were the twins, Yahweh and Baal Hadad, riding on storm clouds, like their father, throwing lightning bolts at each other, gods of power who did not know how to share.

They called Me Mother of All Living, the First Thought. They called Me Queen of Heaven, Lady of the Sea. As El and I separated more and more from our One Being, becoming distinct in our Creation, We became partners, King and Queen, and We were given many names. I would speak wisdom into his ear and El would act. I counseled all my children, taught them to manage their realms, to get along with each other. With Astarte, I taught the people the sacred sexual rituals, taught the women how to embody Me, the feminine, and taught the men to embody El, the masculine. In states of ecstasy, We would create more people, bring more life to the land and the crops.

For this, they called Me Qadesh, the Holy One, and made statues and figurines of Me that they would place on every high hill and under every green tree. With Anat, I would ride into battle, naked on a roaring lion, blood dripping from my teeth, ready to rip the enemy to shreds, protecting my pride of lions, my children. For this, they called Me Lion Lady. With Yahweh and Baal, the twins, I would cast rain to the ground, bringing forth life from the dry dust at our feet. We showed the people how to plant and harvest in seasonal cycles, how to feed themselves without our help. We showed them how to combine the chaste tree with crown daisy and cannabis leaves, to partake in visions where they could see us directly. For this, they called Me Asherah, Goddess of the Trees.

For millennia, I counseled my children, I tended to the land, I cared for the people. I did not care what they called Me, as they knew who I was: their Mother. But I failed my children. I allowed the gods to expand and grow, to take on their own names and regions, to become beloved by their chosen people. I never expected Yahweh, my powerful lightning child, my child who never liked to be called by his own name, to turn against us all and try to rule alone. Yahweh took on his father's name, claiming that he was the supreme Creator. El allowed this, knowing his son would one day take his throne, as has always happened and will always happen in the realms of the gods. El retreated to the dew that floats high above the earth, leaving the people to themselves. I did not follow Him there. I knew the people needed us, needed Me, and I would not abandon them. So Yahweh took Me on as his partner, his beloved, his Asherah, and We reigned the People of El, *Isra-el*, peacefully for a time while the other gods took care of their own people. They fashioned a stone to represent Yahweh and placed it in their temples. They fashioned a simple tree, a pole, to represent Me, and placed it beside the stone.

We spoke into our peoples' ears, visited them in dreams, in the sacred act of sexual ecstasy, or when tasting the visionary fruit of the acacia tree. They baked cakes for Me and poured libations into the ground. They sacrificed animals to Him and burned the flesh in his honor. We counseled the people in temples, in rituals, on every high hill, and under every green tree.

But this was not enough for Yahweh. He wanted more, more power, more for Himself. He challenged Baal, his own twin brother, with the intent to destroy Him and his power, to take his people for Himself. Through a human named Elijah, He tried to convince the people that all their problems came from worshiping his brother in his own regions. Elijah told them to turn away from Baal, Astarte, and Anat, told them that Yahweh was really El, the Father of the Gods, the one that was once a part of Me. He told them it was a sin to worship Me, that they should put aside their cakes and libations and forget my name forever. Yahweh won this battle.

It was a mistake. Elijah and his followers had gained a taste of power, and it was like blood in Anat's mouth. The kings fought with each other, like Yahweh had with Baal, exiling each other, killing each other, stealing each other's women, children, and stories. These men weakened our people so much that they were exiled from their land. This broke Yahweh's heart. I would find Him at rest but not sleeping, refusing to eat. Lightning moved under his eyes and his brow became white as meadowsweet.

I was angry with Him for not listening to Me, for agreeing to let his people stop worshiping Me. But I would never stop loving my son, no matter what sins He committed. So We tried again to help the people, together this time. We followed them wherever they went, helped them to remember where they came from, to reach out for the comfort of our love in foreign trees and sand. We taught them they did not need the land to be our people.

But the powerful had learned how to speak with the charm of Astarte and the viper sharpness of Anat, and they were not finished with Me. They told the people to destroy what little I'd become to them, a few poles in the temples, having forgotten altogether what I look like. They told the people to murder the followers of my daughters, to turn their temples into blood-soaked latrines. They made the false promise that worshiping Yahweh alone would save them. Yahweh had promised too much. He had underestimated the will of his people to destroy themselves and each other, to put power above love and even survival.

My heart was also broken, and I grew tired. I withdrew my blessings from the people as they erased Me from their history books, changing my many names to nothing but a reference to a tree or a grove, with no trace of the goddess I'd always been, Yahweh's Mother, his partner, Queen of his kingdom. We allowed the people to understand their own world the way they wanted to, without Me, and watched them suffer through exile after exile. Yahweh had gained power, but at the cost of his family, his people's Mother, his Asherah. And yet, even still, some remembered. They felt Me in their blood, in their bones, in the breath of the wildwood. They would listen to my voice in the rustle of the willow trees, taste Me in the fruit of the date palm, remember the echo of my name while chewing the leaves of the chaste tree. I reminded them that I was within them, that they had power, that the Goddess had always been as powerful as the God and more so. And I would hold them, whisper my wisdom into their ears, letting them know I had never really left them, that I never really would.

And one day a Son appeared, a human man claiming to be the child of Yahweh. The cycle was to continue once again, with the Son taking the throne of the Father. This Son remembered Me, too, though not by my name. He saw Me in the women around Him and helped to give them power, to let them speak my wisdom through their mouths. He tried to bring Me back. And still, the powerful tried to quiet Him, to quiet Me, again, as they had done for so long. They wrote new books about this Son of God, and some of them wrote about Me, too. But these writings, especially the teachings of women, were cut out of the books, hidden away in clay jars, buried for some future time when the world might welcome Me again.

And I can feel that time is coming. I can hear my name spoken in quiet corners, a flame in the belly of those who can still feel Me. They close their eyes in a grove of trees, not knowing why it's sacred, not knowing my name, but feeling Me there with them, in the caress of the breeze on their skin, the scent of oak and poppies in the air. As they are a part of Me, I am a part of them, always. He is Yahweh, but I am Asherah.

ASHERAH: GODDESS OF TREES

Asherah has been around since long before the Bible, long before Judaism even existed. The earliest evidence of her worship is an asherah pole, a symbolic image of a tree representing her, that was found in Israel, dating all the way back to 4540 BCE – pretty much the beginning of civilization.

She was worshiped throughout the Near East by different names, but is best known as the Canaanite Asherah, the consort of the supreme creator god El, and the mother of many gods including Baal, Astarte, Anat, Mot, and, yes, Yahweh, the god of the Old Testament. Some believe the creation story in Genesis is about El and Asherah creating the world together.

Asherah is clearly present in the Bible for those who are looking for her. It's apparent from the text itself that it was normal for people to worship many gods and goddesses until the trouble began around the eighth century BCE, and we see some of this drama unfold around Jezebel. Much of the Hebrew Bible was written long after the events it describes, intended to create history and meaning for the people of Israel, Yahweh's people, who eventually became the Jewish culture and religion. Its writers generally take the view that the problem all the time was that the people were worshiping other gods alongside Yahweh, and if they could just commit, they'd stop running into trouble.

Not everyone agreed with this, of course. In the Book of Jeremiah (44:18), the people explain to the prophet:

"We're going to go right on offering sacrifices to the Queen of Heaven and pouring out drink offerings to her, keeping up the traditions set by our ancestors, our kings and government leaders in the cities of Judah and the streets of Jerusalem in the good old days. [...] the moment we quit sacrificing to the Queen of Heaven and pouring out offerings to her, everything fell apart. We've had nothing but massacres and starvation ever since."[9]

The Queen of Heaven is a common name for a goddess, often used for Asherah as well as, much later, the Virgin Mary. Despite the best attempts of the prophets to encourage the sole worship of Yahweh, the people did not want to give up their goddess.

The phrase "Yahweh and his Asherah" appears in the Hebrew Bible and several ancient inscriptions found by archaeologists, implying they were normally worshiped together. Ancient temples would have the stone, for Yahweh, and the pole, for Asherah, right next to each other. It would have been strange, in fact, for any god to rule without a feminine consort.

For reasons we may never fully understand, those in power – those who could read and write – were invested in the concept of monotheism, worshiping Yahweh alone. When the Hebrew Bible was translated into Greek around the second century BCE, the goddess was literally overwritten: the words "Asherah" and "asherim" are replaced by words like "wood" or "grove." Eventually, the strategies to erase the goddess and the other gods worked pretty well. But it didn't last: here we are, thousands of years later, remembering her name: Asherah.

WORKING WITH ASHERAH: DIVINE FEMININE WISDOM

In Canaanite mythology, Asherah was often understood to be a counselor to the other gods, especially her consort El, and then Yahweh. She was also the creatrix of the universe, and in some traditions, she was the Word itself that created the world. Considering her most common icon was an asherah pole, a symbolic representation of the tree, some think Asherah represents the Tree of Life itself.

Asherah is sometimes conflated with her daughters Anat and Astarte, to the point that some consider them a triplicate, three aspects of the same goddess. Astarte is likely a form of Inanna and Ishtar, Queens of Heaven who later influenced the Greek Aphrodite and Roman Venus.

Asherah is the epitome of divine feminine resilience. She was powerful and beloved for a long time before she was exiled, and in an era where wisdom is no longer locked up in the writings of the elite few who could read and write, she's coming back to life. Maybe there's some wisdom in staying quiet for a while, in letting people think what they want, while knowing the truth in your heart. The divine feminine has always figured out a way to stay powerful, even if that has meant being exiled for a while.

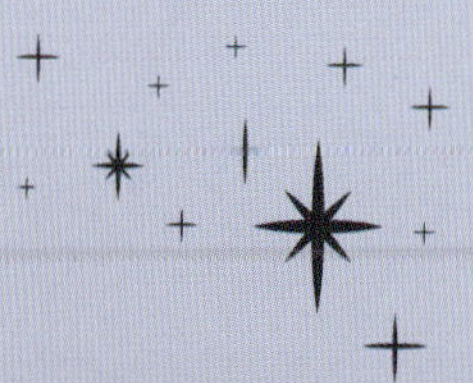

YAHWEH'S NAME

In the earliest Biblical texts, God is referred to as "El," the name of the Canaanite father god, and namesake of the people of Isra-el. When Moses encounters him in the form of a burning bush (an episode many people now think was essentially a psychedelic journey), he reveals himself as Yahweh, not really a name, but a word that means something like "I am who I am." This god took on many of the characteristics of El and his rival god Baal, all of whom would ride on clouds and throw thunderbolts, not unlike Zeus, the Greek King of the Gods.

Yahweh was, then, a son of El and Asherah, a brother to Baal (though the idea that they were twins is my invention). Some also suspect that Yahweh is actually an Egyptian god, Amun, who had something of a heretical desire to be worshiped alone, without all the other gods of his pantheon. According to this theory, the pre-Judaic people were highly influenced by Egyptian people and belief systems - and maybe even originated from there. The (much later) writers of the Bible saw Egypt as the enemy, and wanted to hide that lineage, so they obscured this possible "true name" of Yahweh - Amun. Yahweh is unusual in that his name is hidden, and even to this day there is something of a taboo in saying his various titles out loud.

There's also a little mythology that could support this theory of Egyptian origin. The Egyptian goddess Isis is said to have tricked Amun one day into revealing his true name to her. Within Hebrew mythology, Lilith, Adam's first wife, rejected the paradise of Eden, escaping only because she happened to know "the true name of god" which gave her power over him. Perhaps Yahweh's true name is Amun, known only to the goddesses of the divine feminine.

MEDITATION WITH ASHERAH:

The Wisdom of the Trees

Asherah has been many things, but above all she has always been a goddess of the trees. If possible, do this meditation in a grove of trees, under the shade of a favorite tree, or perhaps with a simple twig or branch, a representation of the essence of trees you can hold in your hands.

Consider the land that you are on and the trees that you know in this region, your relationship with their seasonal blooms or evergreen scent, the maple sap or the fruits you love to taste. Then consider the desert trees of Asherah, the powerful plants that grew in arid regions, strong enough to feed the people. Think of the date palm, the sycamore fig, the willow, myrtle, juniper, and oak. Take a deep breath in as if you could smell the fragrance of these trees.

Now imagine roots growing down from your own body into the earth, drawing up nourishment from this ancient land that is so much older than you, that remembers Asherah in her heyday, long before she was exiled. Imagine her wisdom growing up through these deep ancient roots, rising into your body, filling you with her power, her resilience, and her wisdom.

Listen to the divine spark within, your own inner knowing, as you embody Asherah herself. Ask questions if you like. If there are no questions, that's fine, just be with her, with the Asherah in your body, represented in the wisdom of the trees. Tune into your inner and outer hearing, listening for the sweet subtle vibration of the trees or the wood in your hand. Trust what the trees know.

When this feels complete for you, thank Asherah for her power and resilience, for being with you and within the essence of the trees that are still here, growing all along, whether or not anyone knew they were there.

CONCLUSION

The divine feminine has had many names across the ages. Once, she was supreme across the world, often upheld as more powerful than the divine masculine. Today, she is somewhat hidden, outcast, ridiculed, even feared. We might have forgotten our ancestors' ways, the ancient names for the gods and goddesses that were once a part of our daily lives. But we want them. We crave them. Something in us knows they are still there.

Meeting the Witch, the Healer, the Priestess, and the Outcast feels like peering beyond the veil, seeing reality through histories that have been actively and purposefully hidden from us to make sure we forget our own power.

I am still, in many ways, the Witch I became when I was a teen. This has woven itself into my work as a Healer, and writing this book has made me feel like a Priestess, one who shares the numinous with those who want to know. I am no stranger to the Outcast to this day, perhaps especially because I read tarot and cast spells and can't stop talking about how the goddess was erased from the Bible.

Experiencing these tales is, in a sense, a reclaiming of the land, a re-storying of the spirit of the natural elements these deities once ruled. In remembering them, we remember the date palms of ancient Israel, the bluebell-filled woodlands of Britain, the sweet, fresh river waters of Africa, and the cold, northern winds of Scandinavia. No matter where our ancestors are from, we are of the land we live on: we eat of it, we drink of it, we bathe in its waters, and we need its stories. If these stories bring us back to our physical bodies, our relationship with the land we depend on for our survival, maybe we can also re-story our relationship with the divine feminine, with each other, and with the world around us. The Witch, the Healer, the Priestess, and the Outcast will be by our side as we do.

BIBLIOGRAPHY

Bowen, Natasha, *Skin of the Sea* (Penguin Random House Children's Books, 2021)

Cath Maige Tuired: The Second Battle of Mag Tuired (Irish Texts Society, 1982)

Ehrenreich, Barbara and English,. Deirdre, *Witches, Midwives, and Nurses: A History of Women Healers* (ReadHowYouWant.com, 2010)

Federici, Silvia, *Caliban and the Witch* (Autonomedia, 2004)

Frawley, David, *Tantric Yoga and the Wisdom Goddesses: Spiritual Secrets of Ayurveda* (Lotus Press, 1994)

Freeman, Philip, *Celtic Mythology: Tales of Gods, Goddesses, and Heroes* (Oxford University Press, 2017)

Fuller-Shafer, Kelsey A., *Norse Mythology: The Gods, Goddesses, and Heroes Handbook, from Vikings to Valkyries, an Epic Who's Who in Old Norse Mythology* (Adams Media, 2023)

Gimbutas, Marija, *The Living Goddesses* (University of California Press, 2001)

Hazleton, Lesley, *Jezebel: The Untold Story of the Bible's Harlot Queen* (Doubleday, 2007)

Holy Bible (New International Version) (Zondervan, 2008)

Karade, Baba Ifa, *The Handbook of Yoruba Religious Concepts* (Red Wheel Weiser, 1994)

Kempton, Sally, *Awakening Shakti: The Transformative Power of the Goddesses of Yoga* (Sounds True, 2013)

Kinsley, David R., *Tantric Visions of the Divine Feminine: The Ten Mahāvidyās.* (Motilal Banarsidass, 1998)

Murphy, Joseph M., Sanford, Moi-Moi, *Òsun Across the Waters: A Yoruba Goddess in Africa and the Americas* (Indiana University Press, 2001)

Ni, Xueting Christine, *From Kuan Yin to Chairman Mao: The Essential Guide to Chinese Deities* (Red Wheel/Weiser, 2018)

Nilsen, Tim, *Helheim – Realm of the Goddess Hel: The Ruler of Life and Death in Norse Mythology* (2024)

Oliver, Cheyenne, "Which Witch? Morgan Le Fay as Shapeshifter and English Perceptions of Magic in Arthurian Legend" (Masters' thesis, Florida Atlantic University, 2015)

Peterson, Eugene (trans.), *The Message Bible* (Gardners Books, 2001)

Picknett, Lynn and Prince, Clive, *When God Had a Wife: The Fall and Rise of the Sacred Feminine in the Judeo-Christian Tradition* (Inner Traditions/Bear, 2019)

Sedgwick, Icy, *Rebel Folklore: Empowering Tales of Spirits, Witches and Other Misfits from Anansi to Baba Yaga* (Dorling Kindersley, 2023)

Strand, Sophie, *The Madonna Secret* (Inner Traditions/Bear, 2023)

Sturluson, Snorri, *The Prose Edda* (TGC Press, 2024)

Weber, Courtney, *Hekate: Goddess of Witches* (Red Wheel Weiser, 2021)

Yü, Chün-fang, *Kuan-yin: The Chinese Transformation of Avalokiteśvara* (Columbia University Press, 2001)

OTHER SOURCES

PODCASTS

A Little Juju
Africa's Untold Stories
Afro Mythos
Allegory Story
An Audio Guide to Ancient Rome
Bible and Archaeology
Bible Stories
Bledsoe Said So
Catholic Stuff You Should Know
Chthonia Podcast with Brigid Burke
Dawn of the New Earth
For the Love of Yoga with Nish the Fish
Forbidden History
Governed by God
History for Weirdos
History Uncovered
Intuitive Awakening
Kalliope's Sanctum with Sylvia Linsteadt on Rhea Silvia
Magical, Mystical Journeys on Guan Yin featuring Dr. Emily Wu
Men, This Way, featuring Sophie Strand
Misquoting Jesus with Bart D. Ehrman
Mythical Monsters
Mythical Musings
Mythology: A Spotify Original from Parcast
Mythos
Myths and Legends
MythVision
Nature Folklore
Norse Mythology: The Unofficial Guide
Once Upon a Goddess
Only the Strongest Roots See the Light
Origins Explained
Sci Fi Tales
Sit a Spell: Folklore and Mythology
Spirits
Story Archaeology with Chris Thompson and Isolde Carmody
Styx and Bones
The Ancients
The Ashe Shop, with Ashley
The Faerytale Apothecary
The Goddess Divine
The Goddess Project
The Goddess, The Witch, and the Womb
The History of Ancient Greece
The History of Yoruba Land
The Jesus Witch
The Partial Historians
Unrefined Women
Wicked Women, with Gretchen Upshaw, Adrianna Canabal, and Sarah Drago
Women of Controversy: Womanica

COURSE

Myths as Maps: a course with Sophie Strand, www.sophiestrand.com

ENDNOTES

1 This story is influenced by *Oshun Across the Waters* and retellings by Ashley (Ashe Shop podcast), Joseph Baba Ifa and Erica Oshun Poroye (Our Roots Podcast), and Juju Bae (A Little Juju Podcast).

2 Sourced largely from the *Cath Maige Tuired*, especially the translation by Elizabeth Gray.

3 Quoted in Lesley Hazleton's *Jezebel: The Untold Story of the Bible's Harlot Queen*.

4 Ahab's words, quoted from 1 Kings 20:11 (Hazleton).

5 A famous Biblical curse, 1 Kings 19 (Hazleton).

6 Sarcasm from 2 Kings 9 (Hazleton).

7 I was introduced to this tradition through yoga teachers including Eric Stoneberg, who learned under David Kinsley, a scholar of Tantra.

8 His text, the *Prose Edda*, draws on the poetry and songs of the *Poetic Edda*.

9 This passage quoted from *The Message Bible* translation of the Holy Bible, by Eugene Peterson.

ACKNOWLEDGMENTS

Huge thanks to Lizzie Kaye for being so willing to listen to my ideas and give me the opportunity to immerse myself in these goddesses and tell their stories. Sam Staddon, Victoria Allen, Jane Trollope, Sophie Seager, and everyone at Verbena have been wonderful to work with and have all been so important in bringing this book to life. I am incredibly grateful to the illustrator Nadia Murash for taking on this project and showing it such passion and beauty. My agent Robert Lecker is a friend, an editor, a teacher, a mentor, and a cheerleader, and I'm so grateful to have him on my team.

Thank you to everyone who sat in front of a microphone and shared their knowledge and experience through the many podcasts I listened to, especially Chthonia, Story Archeology, Afro Mythos, A Little Juju, the Ashe Shop, Mythology, Spirits, The Ancients, and Sylvia Lindsteadt's version of Rhea Silvia's story on the Kalliope's Sanctum podcast. Sophie Strand was incredibly influential through both her writing and her oral teaching.

Thank you to Olivia Davies, Megan Laven, Mary Moore, Emilee Nimetz, Natalie Rousseau, Tracy Stefanucci, the brilliant minds and hearts in my Coven, my parents Jane and Mike, and my husband Robert Beal for listening to my stories, sharing resources, and giving me ideas. Deep thanks to the ancients, the lands, and all the stories that survived somehow, despite the best attempts to erase them.

ABOUT THE AUTHOR

Julie Peters is a counseling therapist and tarot reader living and working on Plains Cree land in Treaty 6 territory, also known as Edmonton, Alberta, Canada. She is a staff writer for *Spirituality and Health Magazine* and has dozens of guided meditations on the Insight Timer meditation app. Julie is the author of *Secrets of the Eternal Moon Phase Goddesses: Meditations on Desire, Relationships, and the Art of Being Broken*, the Canada Book Award-winning *Want: 8 Steps to Recovering Desire, Passion, and Pleasure After Sexual Assault*, *The Full Moon Yearbook: A Year of Ritual and Healing Under the Full Moon* and the first book in this series, *Maiden, Warrior, Mother Crone: Divine Feminine Archetypes in Modern Life*. Learn more at www.juliepeters.ca.

INDEX

A VERBENA BOOK

Verbena is an imprint of David and Charles, Ltd, Suite A, Tourism House, Pynes Hill, Exeter, EX2 5WS

First published in the UK and USA in 2025

A catalogue record for this book is available from the British Library.

ISBN-13: 9781446316566 paperback
ISBN-13: 9781446316696 EPUB

This book has been printed on paper from approved suppliers and made from pulp from sustainable sources.

Printed in China through Leo Paper Product ltd. for:
David and Charles, Ltd
Suite A, Tourism House, Pynes Hill, Exeter, EX2 5WS

10 9 8 7 6 5 4 3 2 1

Publishing Director: Ame Verso
Senior Commissioning Editor: Lizzie Kaye
Publishing Manager: Jeni Chown
Editor: Victoria Allen
Copy Editor: Julie Trollope
Designer: Sam Staddon
Pre-press Designer: Susan Reansbury
Illustrations: Nadia Murash
Production Manager: Beverley Richardson

David and Charles publishes high-quality books on a wide range of subjects. For more information visit www.davidandcharles.com.

Follow us on Instagram by searching for @verbena_books and @dandcbooks.

Layout of the digital edition of this book may vary depending on reader hardware and display settings.